APOLOGY AGAINST THEDORE

St. Cyril of Alexandria,
Patriarch of Alexandria

Translated by: D.P. Curtin

Dalcassian Publishing Company
PHILADELPHIA, PA

Copyright @ 2008 Dalcassian Publishing Company

All rights reserved. No part of this publication may be reproduced, distributed, or transmitted in any form or by any means, including photocopying, recording, or other electronic or mechanical methods, without the prior written permission of the publisher, except in the case of brief quotations embodied in critical reviews and certain other non-commercial uses permitted by copyright law. For permission request, write to Dalcassian Publishing Company at dalcassianpublishing at gmail.com

ISBN: 979-8-8689-9117-2 (Paperback)

Library of Congress Control Number:
Author: Curtin, D.P. (1985-)

Printed by Ingram Content Group, 1 Ingram Blvd, La Vergne, Tennessee

First printing edition 2008.

APOLOGY AGAINST THEODORE

Cyril, to the most reverend and beloved brother and priest Evptius, greetings in the Lord.

I read what your holiness transmitted to me some time ago, and I marveled at the affection and sincerity of charity in Christ; but I think it necessary to exclaim now also in the most appropriate manner, what is written in the book of Proverbs: Brother helped by brother, like a well-fortified city (Prov. 18:19). And indeed, it seems to me that the charity of the divine Scriptures has been most honored with praise, and rightly so, since it has in itself the fullness of the law (Rom. 13:10), and its virtues are to be preferred to others, and to the minds of the saints it is seen to be wonderful. That is to say, what we say is not to be filled with mere words, but with evidence from things themselves. For just as the most precious stones, which the Indians say are, not if anyone remembers their beauty, but if they themselves are beautiful, they are to be admired by the eyes of the beholders; thus, from the very examples it appears that the excellent beauty of charity is compared to all goods.

This your reverence makes most, to always observe the footsteps of the saints, and to follow the praises of their well-proven lives. I therefore received, that I might know the affection of your sanctity even now, the tome which was transmitted, which is said to have been composed against the anathemas of Theodoretus Cyrus: for so I hear that town is called. When I had read this, I gave the greatest thanks to God, and did not cease to say: Lord, deliver my soul from unjust lips and from a deceitful tongue (Ps. 19:2).

For I found that slanders were brought to me everywhere and in every chapter. I was therefore surprised that a man who was not a stranger to literature, as some have reported of him, and perhaps endowed with not a moderate knowledge of sacred literature, should have been so ignorant of the power of chapters, that I suspected that he had been gratified by a false ignorance of strange desires; that is to say, lest it should appear to us to be at random, and to draw it down without any color: since, above all, there is nothing at all difficult, nothing obscure in our sayings, unless my opinion deceives me, nothing that is difficult to understand. But when it was necessary, although we had already written about these before, to reply to him also in a few words, so that no one might think that we had recanted the convictions, I proceeded to answer as brevity as the matter would permit.

Indeed, the Scriptures have been most fitting for him, since he has divine knowledge of the Scriptures, and wishing to discuss with us about the sacred mysteries, he should have made mention only of the sacred letters, and not of uttering curious and sordid fables; Hence we also marveled at this excessive knowledge of his: for it appears that he was not ignorant of the evil of discord, because of his deep and immense learning, nor Parides the son of Priam.

For in one letter after another: Moreover, not only did he assert these things; but he also ventured to anathematize those who refused to comply with his blasphemies. If, however, these inventions are his own, and no longer some enemy of the truth has thrown them into the midst as if written by him, like that which is in fables, the evil of discord, which kindles the flame.

It is true that we, having sent them in the meantime, persist in our purpose.

THE FIRST ANATHEMA

Let him not confess that God is really Emmanuel, and therefore that the Holy Virgin is Θεοτόκον: for she gave birth carnally to the Word of God made flesh; let him be.

CRIMINATION OF HERETICS.

But we who follow the evangelical tradition do not call God the Word, made flesh by nature, and turned into flesh. Indeed, God is irreversible and unchangeable, of whom the Prophet David also says: But you are the same, and your years will not fail (Psal. 11:28). That Paul was said to be the greatest preacher of the truth about the Son, he asserted in his letter to the Hebrews (Heb. 1:11); and elsewhere through the Prophet God says: I am, I am, and I have not been changed (Malach. 3:6). Therefore, if God is unconvertible and unchangeable, He cannot suffer conversion and exchange; and if it is impossible for the invertible to be converted, God the Word was not made flesh and converted, but assumed flesh and dwelt among us according to the words of the Gospels. And the divine Paul himself, explaining this in his letter to the Philippians, says: Feel this in yourselves, that even in Christ the Son, who, being in the form of God, did not think of robbery, that he might be equal to God, but emptied himself, taking the form of a servant (Phil. II, 5).

It appears, therefore, from what has been said, that the form of God is not converted into the form of a servant; but remaining what he was, he took the form of a servant. Therefore, if God the Word was not made flesh, but assumed living and rational flesh, he was not himself born of the Virgin by nature, conceived, and fashioned, and formed, and thence began, that he might be, receiving him who is before the ages, and God, and always with God, and adhering to the Father, and to be known and worshiped with the Father, when he had fashioned a temple for himself in the womb of a virgin, he adhered to the created, and conceived, and formed, and born. For this reason, we also call the holy Virgin Θεοτόκον, not because nature gave birth to God, but because she brought forth man conjoined to God, who had formed him.

The whole of this paragraph is referred to in the fifth synod, among those of Theodoret, against Saint Cyril, which were condemned with anathema; but it is his abomination that he contradicts Saint Cyril in that part in which the reason for faith was laid, namely, that the blessed Virgin gave birth to the Word made flesh, and not only to man conjoined to God.

But if it is not man who was formed in the womb of the Virgin, but God the Word, who is before the ages; therefore, God the Word is the work of the Holy Spirit. For what is born in her, says Gabriel, is from the Holy Spirit (Matthew 1:20). But if the only-begotten Word of God is uncreated, and of the same substance as the Father, it is not the work of the Holy Spirit. But if the Word did not form God in the womb of the Virgin Spirit, it remains for us to understand that the form of a servant is formed and fabricated by nature.

But since he was not so much in the form of a servant, but having the inhabitant of the temple, God the Word, according to the voice of Paul: For in him, he says, all the fullness of the Godhead was pleased to dwell bodily (Colossians 1:19); not only ἀνθρωποτόκον, but also Θεοτόκον we call the holy Virgin; ἀντρωποτόκον, because of fiction and formation; Θεοτόκον, because of ἕνωσιν, calling: therefore the child that was born was called Emmanuel; nor God separated from human nature, nor man naked of divinity. For Emmanuel signifies that God is with us, according to the words of the Gospels; But God is with us, and he signifies him who was taken from us for us, and he shows God the Word, which he took. Therefore, Emmanuel was a child because of God, who took him; and the Virgin Θεοτόκος because of the conjunction of God in the form of a servant; nor was God the Word turned into flesh: but the form of God took the form of a servant.

THE ORTHODOX RESPONSE

We have accused many and often those who refuse to confess that God is really Emmanuel, and that the Holy Virgin is Θεοτόκον, because she gave birth to the Word of God in the flesh, when it was made flesh, that is, man. But truly he who accuses us of so rightly speaking, if he does not know that God really is Emmanuel; if the Word of God, according to the Scriptures, was not born carnally from the holy Virgin, made flesh; why did he not cry out more openly: What are you doing, good man? You spew out strange words, dogmas of the barrel of truth. God is not truly Immanuel, nor the holy Virgin Θεοτόκος, so that even we who cry out and say these things, wisely opposing what was said by the divine Scriptures, and the tradition of the apostolic and evangelical faith, and the confession of the holy Fathers, who in their time gathered at Nicaea, we would persuade them that, when they uttered it, it was neither right nor honest to try to argue with what we had said; rather, he hastens to resist the divine Scriptures.

But the prudent and persuasive negotiator, having passed over those things which it was necessary and necessary for him to say, and when he had touched none of these, he took a completely different course. let it be, as if this were true, that he either feels, or affirms, that it is anathema.

Let him hear, then, who does not know how to respond to another's prayer: man, you are vain in your discourses without reason, and you resist an opinion or an opinion that is hateful to us. For we know, too, that not even a shadow of the conversion of that divine and excellent nature is perpetuated, and that the Word of God has not migrated into the nature of the flesh, deposited by the Deity.

But when he mentions that the form of the servant was taken from the form of God, let him teach us that without substances alone and by themselves the forms agree with each other. But this, I think, he will also confess that it is not so: for species were not only without substances, and forms met with each other through the dispensation of ἕνωσιν; but the meeting of the things themselves, or of the substances, took place, so that the system of inhumanity might be believed to have really taken place. Therefore, even if we say that the Word of God became flesh, we do not say that confusion, nor mixing, nor again conversion, or exchange happened to it; but that it is itself joined, by a mysterious and ineffable reason, to the holy body having a rational soul: for whatever is said to be joined, it is not confused, but rather assumes something else for itself.

We affirm, therefore, that the Word of God the Father assumed holy and animate flesh, and that he was truly unconfused, conjoined from the very womb, that indeed he came forth as a man, but that he also remained the true God; therefore, also the holy Virgin is Θεοτόκος. But I think it is superfluous to call her also ἀνθρωποτόκον. For if some were so taken in mind as to say that the nature of the Word came from the flesh, as if it were the source of its origin, and that the beginning of its existence was drawn from it, perhaps they would not seem to do it without some reason, who would show that it ought to be called ἀνθρωποτόκον. But since this kind of opinion is odious to all, it cannot be otherwise understood that Θεοτόκος is a holy Virgin, unless one first believes that he was made flesh, that is, that he was made man, the Word of God the Father (for the naked divinity was not born of a virgin), that for us from this Do those who contend that it should also be called ἀνθρωποτόκον give rise to a contention of profit?

True, as far as it appears, they devised a place for themselves to speak against Christ; for they do not suffer, either to feel or to say, the very Word of God the Father, who was before the ages the Son, in the last times unconfused and irrevocably united, from the womb, having a rational soul in the flesh, and thus to have been a man like us. But just as they mention that one of the saints had an indwelling God, they worry others to feel the same way: not considering that the God of all dwells in us also through the Holy Spirit, as in the holy temples. For it is written: Know ye not that ye are the temple of God, and that the spirit of God dwelleth in you? If then, anyone corrupts the temple of God, God will corrupt him; for the temple of God is holy, which you are (1 Cor. 3:16). But though we are called temples, having God indwelling us through the Spirit; yet we know another way of the mystery, according to Christ: for we say that the flesh is truly united to God the Word, that is, having a rational soul.

But I would gladly consult him whether he truly confesses that the unity of the Word of God and humanity, or of the holy body rationally animated, has been made; or he also, after the example of some, by the mere conjunction of the servile and ἀνυποστάτου form with the ἐνυποστάτῳ divine form, or in another way, by the sole filiation of ὁμωνυμίαν and equality of dignity; or if any other mode of conjunction is meant? But perhaps I am troublesome without cause, and I do not necessarily interrogate for I have his words, and a most open confession; For in the first chapter he said: That is why the child born is called Emmanuel, neither God is separated from human nature, nor man is naked of divinity. It was necessary, indeed, to take care of the subtle exposition of these things, and to take care of them; Moreover, it must be noted. For behold, he himself, expounding on unity, denies that God is separated from human nature by unity, and confesses that he is both God and man at the same time: why then is he not ashamed, rebuking our words?

SECOND ANATHEMA

Let him not confess that the Word of God the Father is united to the flesh by substance, and that Christ is one with his own flesh, that is to say, the same God and man at the same time; let him be.

CRIMINATION OF HERETICS.

Indeed, we confess one Christ, obeying the divine traditions of the apostles, and call him God and man for the sake of ἕνωσιν. We completely ignore the truth of ἕνωσιν by substance, as being new and alien from the divine Scriptures and the Fathers who interpreted them.

And here, too, the whole passage was reported and condemned in the fifth synod, on the ground that it rejected ἕνωσιν καθ' ὑπόστασιν, the confession of which is the only, undoubted, and clear rule of good feeling for fraud. Hence in canon 13 anathema is said to him who defended the impious writings of Theodoret, which were against the right faith and against the first holy synod of Ephesus, and Saint Cyril; and the twelve chapters of it, he expounded, and all that he wrote for the impious Theodore and Nestorius, and for others who knew the same things as the aforementioned Theodore and Nestorius, defending them and their impiety, and for this reason calling the teachers of the Church impious, who they confess to the flesh, etc.

But if he who discovers these things wants to say ἕνωσιν by a substance in which the divinity and the flesh have been mixed, we will contradict it with all zeal, and we will be convinced of blasphemy. For it is necessary that confusion should follow confusion; but the confusion that follows takes away the property of nature: for things that are mixed do not keep what they were before; but to say that about God the Word and about the seed of David is most outrageous. But it is necessary to obey the Lord who shows the two natures, and who says to the Jews: Dismantle this temple, and in three days I will rebuild it (John 2:19). But if the mixture had taken place, neither God would have remained God, nor would the temple have been recognized as a temple, but God would have been a temple, and the temple God: for this is what the reason for the mixture requires; and it is not right for the Lord to say to the Jews: Dismantle this temple, and I will rebuild it in three days. For it was necessary to say thus: Release me, and I will rise again in three days; for indeed there would have been confusion and confusion; but now he shows that both the temple is to be dissolved and God is to be resurrected. Superfluous, therefore, by the substance ἕνωσις, which, as I think, they use as a mixture; but it is sufficient to say ἕνωσιν, which also shows the properties of the natures, and commands Christ to be worshiped as one.

THE ORTHODOX RESPONSE

Behold, again this noble barbarian, seizing the opportunity of cursing from the smallest causes, criticizes the saying which we have said by substance, and defines it as unusual, and affirms that it was made by us in a new manner; nor does he consider that the force of words, opposing the truth to the cunning of impious heretics, destroys that which seems to oppose it.

Nestorius, therefore, everywhere voiding the generation of the Word of God according to the flesh, and establishing for us the only unity of dignities, and saying that man was honored by being united to God by sonship ὁμωνυμίᾳ; it was necessary that, acting against his words, we should say that they were made by the substance of ἕνωσιν. Now this discourse signifies nothing else, except this only, that the nature, or substance, of the Word, that is, the Word itself, truly united to human nature, without all conversion and confusion, as we have often said, is to be understood as one, and that Christ himself is God and man. . .

These words of Cyril are to be accurately noted: We say that the union is made according to ὑπόστασιν; but here the word signifies nothing else, except that only that the nature of the Word, or hypostasis, that is, the Word itself truly united to human nature, etc. For this is the famous sentence of Athanasius and Cyril: 'after the union the incarnated nature of the word of God is one'. For nature is placed as a hypostasis; nor is that peculiar to the Catholics. Even Nestorius himself, if we believe the Fathers of the Fifth Synod, put natures instead of hypostases, when he said: Because of him who clothes, he who is clothed, I worship: because of him who is hidden, I worship him who is visible. God is inseparable from him who appears therefore, I do not separate the honor of him who is inseparable, I separate the natures, but unite in adoration (Serm. 7, no. 37). But Theodoret confuses one voice with the other in the criticism of the consequent anathema, when he says:

And this, as I think, seems to Theodore himself to be saying that God was not separated from human nature, nor was humanity to be understood without divinity. Therefore, we do not say that the forms of the servant and God are conjoined without the substance, nor do we define the common man as being honored by the equality of dignity alone σεφιτῶς conjoined with the Word; but he himself, as I said above, the only begotten Son of God, who truly took on flesh, which had a rational soul, became man, yet so that he also remained God.

But that man, vehement in his speech, and most active in his thought, defines a mixture to be signified by this kind of expression, and dares to say, and places those things which happen from the mixture of natures in the middle, as if we were ignorant of whether perhaps, he is boasting of a certain insolence, and thinks that there is no one else but himself. to be able to propagate speech as much as he will; if only he proposed to himself that what was said by no one, as if it were truly said, that something might appear to be among those who do not know how to discern, who are vain talkers and liars, and who keep the right way of truth, and practice prudent and necessary discourses.

I indeed thought, I confess, from the beginning, that he was not at all ignorant of the power of the chapters themselves, but pretended to be ignorant, and in this some were gratified; but now I found that he really did not know him.

THE THIRD ANATHEMA

If, in one Christ, he divides substances after unity, and joins them together by conjunction alone according to dignity, or authority, or dominion, and not more by a certain agreement, which is made, through the natural ἕνωσιν; let him be.

CRIMINATION OF HERETICS.

Obscure, indeed, of the words, and the dim opinion; but in the case of the pious, their madness is plain. For whom it is not clear that conjunction and convention differ nothing? for there is an agreement among those who were divided before. But the most prudent generator of this kind of words, as if he put opposite words that were compatible with him: for it is not necessary, he says, to connect substances by conjunction; but by combination and natural agreement, either perhaps not knowing what to say, or knowingly blaspheming.

For nature is something imperious, and compelling to act, not by will. But what I say is such: We are hungry by nature, not enduring this by will, but by necessity; and if it were not so, the poor would be freed from begging, having it in their will that they should not starve; we feel naturally, we sleep naturally, we breathe naturally. But all these things, as I have said, are not done by the will: for if any one does not admit any of these things, he will necessarily feel the end of his life. Therefore, if the natural conjunction took place in the servile form, by a certain compelling necessity, God the Word was not joined to the servile form by His clemency, and thus the legislator will be found serving the necessary laws. True, the blessed Paul did not teach us in this way, but on the contrary, namely, that he emptied himself by taking the form of a servant (Phil. 2:6); by saying, he emptied himself, signifying his will. If, therefore, by his choice and will, he is joined to the nature assumed from us, the expression of natural conjunction is superfluous: for it is sufficient to confess ἕνωσιν. ἕνωσις is further taken from the divided, for if there is no division, there will never be ἕνωσις, and he who admits ἕνωσιν also admits a previous division.

Why, then, does he say that substances or natures need not be divided, especially when he knows that the substance of the Word of God was perfect, and that the servile form assumed by him was perfect, and therefore he said substances, and not substance? Therefore, if both natures are perfect, and both have come together in one, that is, the form of God assuming the form of a servant, indeed one person, ἓν μὲν πρόσοπον, and one Son and Christ, the reason of piety demands that they be similarly confessed; but to call two substances united, or natures, is not absurd, but more consequential.

For if we divide the natures in one man, and indeed the mortal, we call the body; but the immortal, the soul; and both, man: it is much more fitting to distinguish the properties of the natures of the assumed God, and the assumed man. We also find the blessed Paul, dividing one and the same man into two men, and simply saying: The more the outer man is corrupted, the more the inner man is renewed (2 Cor. 4:16); simply: For the reader of the law of God according to the inner man (Rom. 7:22); and immediately: Christ dwells in the inner man (Ephesians 3:17). If therefore the apostle divides the natural conjunction of the natures of the same time, why does he accuse those who divide the proper natures of the eternal God and his man, who was assumed in the last times, of impiety? He argues, I say, who teaches us the mixture of other names.

THE ORTHODOX RESPONSE

Observe how that wise man, first of all, lies that our words are dark, and when he himself has a cloudy and confused mind, he says that darkness is so plain to the wise, and the plainest speech.

But it was arbitrarily decided that the agreement, and not the conjunction, should be named, our speech affirms. Then, desiring to display his cleverness, he says that one thing is meant by us, and the same thing is meant, whether we say that an agreement or a conjunction has been made. But in this place also I admire the keenness of his mind: for perhaps he alone learned what was never unknown to anyone; and this is so far-fetched, that even to those who are completely alienated from secular learning and literature, it seems very familiar; yea, even to those who have heard only of fables, they have arrived at a light and uncertain knowledge.

Admiring therefore his teaching, I say this to him: Or at least wake up, as if from drunkenness or sleep, who strive to open such a great mouth on us; and observe with precision and acuteness the mystery of unity which is said of Christ. Some make a slander of this unity, by transferring the sentences of the sacred letters into what pleases them; but they contend that man is conjoined to God by σεφιτῶς, according only to dignity, or authority, and according to filiation ὀμωνυμίαν. This anathema fights against the belief, and so resists the novelties of profane words. Indeed, he affirms that the Word was united by nature, that is, not by relation, but by truth, having a reasonable soul in the flesh; and in no way should it be divided, lest we understand two sons, dividing the individual. But he does not understand what is finally natural union, that is, truths which neither confound the natures nor cause a mixture; so that both begin to be something other than what they were, he assumes something childish and frivolous as a proof of what he thinks he is good at.

Finally, he says: If the union has become natural; therefore, the emptying of the Word is not voluntary, but as if from necessity and violence, for nature is an imperious thing. To this anyone will say to him: Hunger, and thirst, and the rest, as you said, are natural infirmities of the flesh, and have their motion in us themselves; because, of course, we have a nature subject to passions. But the divine and mysterious nature of the Word is not capable of necessity, nor of passion, and was compelled by no one at all, not even by himself, to become flesh against his will, or to assume the measure of humanity, and to take hold of Abraham's seed.

But it is not difficult for those who wish to discover that his speech is vehemently ill-advised: for he says absolutely, and beyond doubt, that all natural things are subject to the laws of necessity and as a proof of this he put forward that we should hunger and thirst against our will, our nature provoking us to this, even if one would not (but it was a learned man, and trained in these matters, to see other more solid causes of things, which are worthy to be required by greater prayer); unless perhaps it is false that man is rational by nature. Therefore, he is forced against his will to be reasonable. Then, tell me, is God Almighty not God by nature? Is not nature holy, just, good, life, light, wisdom, and virtue? Is he also against his will, and forced, that is, what he is? But to think in this way is the most certain proof of Vesana's stupidity.

What, then, has falsehood obtained for us as an impregnable and invincible bulwark? and he uses such feeble arguments, that when he hears that a natural union has been made, that is, a true and free from conversion, and an entirely unconfused agreement of substances, he tries to torture the force of the sentences, so that they may be believed to be a little rightly placed? Nor does the vigorous man shudder, recalling that the nature of the Word is subject to inevitable necessity. He emptied himself, not against his will, but willingly becoming man, the only begotten: but not, as you say, he assumed man, giving him conjunction with σεφιτὴν, and honoring him with the grace of sonship, according to us.

Therefore, even if we understand that substances are united, and the Word of God made man and incarnate: and therefore we seem, in some way, to say a natural union, which excludes that, which is not true, but relative, and which we also had through faith and sanctification, because of the divine nature We were participants; indeed, as Paul says: He who clings to the Lord is one Spirit (1 Cor. 6:17); yet we do not subject the impassive and free Word of God to natural necessity and violence.

But the fact that after union we do not want those who have been united to be separated from themselves, unless I am mistaken, is neither criminal at all, nor does it seem culpable, especially since the excellent man Theodoret himself, setting forth one of us as an example, does not allow us to be divided into two; although as far as man's θεωρίαν is concerned, he can be subject to division, namely, because we understand that the soul is one thing by nature, and another by nature proper to flesh. Therefore, investigating more curiously by the same reason, the union which is understood to have been made in Christ, according to the theory of divinity and humanity, we say that the true agreement was made through ἕνωσιν; . But it is criminal to divide what has been gathered once; nor does right reason allow us to separate the one Christ, and the Son, and the Lord into two Sons: for to this knowledge the holy and divine Scripture leads us.

He who is true to the doctrines of the truth has no care at all, and does not labor to learn anything necessary, and which may even moderately benefit him, but only that which may harm him. Nevertheless, when he glories in lying, and boasts that he has cunning in slander, let him hear from us: Why do you glory in malice, who are mighty in iniquity? all day long thy tongue hath thought iniquity (Psal. 6:3).

THE FOURTH ANATHEMA

Let him disperse into two persons, or substances, the words which are in the evangelical or apostolic Scriptures, and which are either spoken of Christ by the saints, or by him of himself, and he may depute these to man, who is understood apart from the Word; indeed, as you divine, only God the Word; let him be.

CRIMINATION OF HERETICS.

These things are also related to the aforesaid: for he wants, as if made by a mixture, that there should be no difference in the words which were said in the sacred Gospels, or in the apostolic books; when especially Arius, and Eunomius, and the rest of the authors of this heresy, he boasted that he was an enemy.

Let the most expert teacher of divine dogmas say, how can he accuse the heretics of blasphemy, deputing the lowly and servile form of words appropriate to God in the Word?

To whom therefore we, who think ourselves different from them, and who confess the Son of the same substance coeternal with God and the Father, the workman of all things, and the maker, and the orderer, and the governor, and the wisest will, and the almighty; wisdom itself. To whom, I say, we should depute these things: God, my God, why have you forsaken me (Matthew 27:46); and that: Father, if it be possible, let this cup pass from me (Matthew 26:39); and: Father, save me from that hour (John 12:27); and that: No one knows that hour, not even the Son of Man (Mark 13:32), and the rest, which were humbly spoken by him, and written about him by the holy apostles? To whom shall we ascribe hunger? Whose fatigue and sleep? Whose ignorance and timidity? Who is it that acted as the helper of the angels? If these are the words of God, how did wisdom ignore them? Or how is wisdom called, which has the defect of ignorance? Or how will it be seen that he has spoken the truth, mentioning that he has all the Father's things, when he has no knowledge of the Father? For, he says, the Father alone knows that day (Matthew 24:36). Or how can the image be the most similar to the parent, who does not have everything of the parent? If he does not lie when he says that he is ignorant, who has thought these things about him? if indeed he knows the day, and wishing to conceal it, he says that he is ignorant: you see what kind of blasphemy results from this; the truth, of course, lies. But who is called truth, which has the opposite of truth? If the truth does not lie, neither is God the Word ignorant of the day which he himself has arranged, in which he is going to judge the world, but he has the knowledge of the Father, because he is a very similar image.

Therefore, it is not ignorance of the Word of God, but of the servile form, which at that time knew as much as the indwelling deity revealed.

And that also almost all that is contained in the paragraph was reported in the fifth synod, as if by Nestorian error, concerning the two sons infected, which Cyril notices.

This can be said of other similar things: for what reason does the Word of God have to say to the Father: Father, if it is possible, let this cup pass from me; yet not as I will, but as thou wilt (Matthew 26:39)? For from this, again, many unreasonable things happen; and first, to disagree with the Father and the Son, and to will one thing for the Father, another for the Son, for he says: Nevertheless, not as I will, but as you will. Then again, we shall see that there is great ignorance in the Son, for he will be found ignorant of saying: If it be possible, let the cup pass. But to say this of God the Word is impious, and full of blasphemy: for he knew most certainly who came for this cause, who voluntarily assumed our nature, who emptied himself, the outcome of the mystery of the dispensation, for which he preached to the holy apostles: Behold, we go up to Jerusalem, and the Son of man will be delivered into the hands of the Gentiles, and will be scourged, and crucified, and rise again on the third day (Matthew 20:1). Who, then, uttered these things, and who rebuked Peter, pleading that it should not happen, how could he have pleaded that it should not happen, if he clearly knew everything that was to come? But how can it not be absurd, that Abraham indeed saw his day many centuries ago, and was congratulated; and that Isaiah also foretold salutary passions, and Jeremiah, and Daniel, and Zechariah, and all the chorus of the prophets; but to ignore it, and to ask for deliverance, and to plead for that which had been beneficial to the salvation of the world? Therefore, these are not the words of the Word of God, but of the form of the servant, which terrified death, because death had not yet been resolved; but God permitted the Word to say these things, giving place to timidity, that the nature of the begotten might appear, and that we should not think δόκημα and φαντασιν, that which was made of Abraham and David, because of the profane heretics, whose faction gave birth to such blasphemy.

Therefore, let us ascribe to God the Word those things which were divinely said or done; but those things which have been humbly spoken, let us fit the form of servants, lest we imitate the blasphemies of Arius and Eunomius.

THE ORTHODOX RESPONSE

Would it not have been much better, I pray thee, to have kept the spirit free from hatred and prejudice, to be able to examine the power of the words? It is true that he does not at all deserve to act; for he turned all things to his will, and said: These are also cognate with the aforesaid: for he wills, as if made by a mixture, that there should be no difference in the words which are written in the holy gospels or apostolic sayings; when especially Arius, and Eunomius, and the rest of the authors of this heresy, boast that he is an enemy. And this he indeed: the truth is so far away, that I may say that the natures were confused with each other, and that they undertook confusion, mixing, and conversion, as far as he is far from feeling right.

But we do not even raise the difference of words: for we know that these things were indeed divinely made, and these things were made humanly; and that these are the most excellent measures of glory; But we assert that it is necessary that they should not be deputed to two persons completely separated from themselves: for if our Lord Jesus Christ is one, there is one faith in him, and one baptism (Eph. 4:5), it will be one and one proper person of him. And if God himself will be at the same time a man, it is certainly fitting that he should speak both divinely and humanly at the same time; since from this his divine and mysterious nature does not in any part become inferior to the majesty of the Father; and that dispensation with the flesh is to be believed, because since he is God, man is also said to have been made next to us.

Therefore, all things are of one Christ, divine and human: for if the Word of God the Father did not become man, he certainly does not speak humanly next to us; But if it is true, he himself shared flesh and blood in the same way as we do, likening himself in all things to his brothers, that is, to us. Why do they most foolishly criticize the most correct system of the dispensation, those who do not tolerate the human voice, and those who, because of the dispensation, are quick to depute humility, as others separate from the Son, servants of the form, as they say?

Now it is foolish to say that they are indeed horrified by the malignity of heretics; but do not want to follow the tradition of the right faith: but it is more valuable, and much more learned, to adapt human voices, not other persons, which is understood as a separate Son, and servants of the form, as they are accustomed to say; but rather to depute the measure of humanity itself: for it was fitting, since God was at the same time man, that the discourses should proceed through both of them.

But I marvel that he also pretends to confess that there is one Christ, that is to say, the same God and man at the same time; then, as if having slipped into oblivion, what he thought he had rightly, he divides one again into two. For he puts the voice of the Savior saying: But of that day or hour no one knows, not even the angels of heaven, not even the Son, but the Father (Mark 13:32). Then, affirming that the Word of God the Father is wisdom, and can foretell all future things, he adds and says: Not then the ignorance of the Word of God, but the form of the servant, which he knew so much at that time; these and other similar things may be said. Therefore, if you do not falsely say one Christ and God the Son, the same God and man at the same time, why do you divide, and are not ashamed to say two sons, unless perhaps they do not appear to be two at all, he who has predetermined knowledge, and he who knows all things, and who let him receive a particular revelation, and who is perfect in wisdom, and knows as much as the Father?

But if he is one and the same, for the reason of the truest union, and not another and another divided and separate, he is entirely his own to know and to be seen not to know. Therefore, he indeed knows divinely, as the wisdom of the Father. But since he is dispensationally subject to the measure of ignorant humanity, and this also he makes familiar with others; although, as we have just said, he is completely ignorant of nothing, but knows all things with the Father.

For what reason, then, is it said that he was hungry, and that he was tired from the journey, since he is life and life-giving, as God, and since he himself is the living bread that comes down from heaven and gives life to the world (John 6:51), and he is the same the Lord of virtues (Psal. 23:10)? Of course, to be truly believed to have been made a man, he thinks that he is human, never going beyond the good of his nature; but keeping them unmoved, in which he always was, and is, and will be.

But he who mentions that the revelation was given to the servant of the indwelling form of God, and that it was predestined, shows us the prophet Emmanuel, and the man of God, and nothing else.

It is indeed a clever thing to say, and he thinks himself impregnable: For if the Word of God, he says, is what he cried out, 'father, if it can be done, this cup will pass from me' (Matthew 26:39).

First, indeed, he disagrees with the Father, and does not rightly refuse to drink the cup; when he knows, he says, that the passion was to be the salvation of the world: therefore, he says, there are no such voices of the Word of God. Let him, therefore, hear against this also from us, who wavers and trembles with such weak reasonings. Therefore, since it seems to you that such voices must be removed from the Word of God, and that they alone should be deputed in the form of a slave, do you not divide one into two sons, and to whom this wise thing seems obscure? For perhaps someone will say, following your arguments, that it is neither likely nor reasonable to refuse the suffering of a servant, and to disagree with the Father, and with him who had dwelt, the Word, when he knew that the suffering would be the salvation of the world, and the cause of life for those who were defeated by death It was therefore necessary, says he, that she herself should be seen as superior in timidity, and obedient to the divine commands. Hence the popular invention of these sentences

Therefore, I certainly confess that all human things are indeed seen as small and insignificant to God the Word; but I require, whose emptiness is understood to have been made, and who willingly endured it. For if, as they say, the form of a servant, or that which was of the seed of David; How and by what reason was it emptied, when it was taken up by God? But if the Word itself, which was in the form and equality of God and the Father, is said to have emptied itself, how again or by what reason was it emptied, if it rejected its emptiness? But the emptiness of God's Word, because he does not know how to suffer conversion, is to act or say something human, because of the dispensational agreement of the flesh.

But even if he became man, reason does not in any way violate the nature of his mystery: for he remained what he was, even though he descended to humanity, for the sake of the world's salvation and life. Therefore, not to two persons, but to one Christ, Son and God, we shall depute the evangelical and holy apostles' voices; neither making his divine nature and glory lesser, for the sake of man, nor denying the dispensation; but believing that the ἐνανθρώπησιν of the Word itself was made for us.

THE FIFTH ANATHEMA

If he dares to say that Christ is a God-born man, and no more truly God, since he is the only Son by nature, because the Word was made flesh, and shared in the same way as we do flesh and blood; let him be.

CRIMINATION OF HERETICS.

We confess that he shared with God the Word in the same way as we do, of blood and flesh and of an immortal soul, by the fact that these things are united to themselves. But we do not say that God the Word became flesh by conversion; but we also accuse those who say this of impiety. But how contrary this is to what has already been said, we may see: for if the Word was made flesh, he certainly did not partake of flesh and blood; but if he has partaken of flesh and blood, as if he had partaken of another besides these: but if the flesh is something else besides himself, he is not himself turned into flesh. Therefore, using the name of communion, we worship indeed one Son, both him who assumed, and him who was assumed; yet we know the difference of natures.

But we do not refuse to say Θεοφόρον, that is, lazy, as it has been said by many holy Fathers: one of whom is the great Basilius, in his speech to Amphilochius concerning the Holy Spirit, who used this name, and in his interpretation of the fifty-ninth psalm. Now we call θεοφόρον, not as I do not know in particular who receives the divine grace, but as all having the united divinity of the Son; for the blessed Paul, explaining this, said: See that no one deceives us, because of philosophy and empty glory, according to the tradition of men, according to the elements of the world, and not according to Christ; because in him dwells all the fullness of the divinity bodily (Colossians 2:8).

THE ORTHODOX RESPONSE

Here, too, it is no trouble to show that he practices vain fables; for we assert that it is not necessary for anyone to call Christ the God-bearing man, lest it be understood that he was among the saints. but rather God made a true man, and the Word of God incarnate.

But he reproaches again what was rightly said, and deceives in various ways, and lies. He says, to tell us, that the Word of God was turned into the nature of flesh, and he drew out reasons from on high, by which he endeavors to prove that the Word of God is not turned. But what I have often said, I will say now also necessarily, since there is no one who says that the divine and immortal nature of the Word was converted into earthly flesh; but let all confess that it is unconvertible. Be spared to expend vain labors, that you may show those who are deceived in nothing, that the Word of God is both invertible by nature, and unchangeable. For whom is so stupid, or taken in his mind, who wants to feel and say something so indecent, and perhaps even abominable to the foolish?

But I greatly wonder that when he affirms everywhere that Emmanuel is God, he is convinced that the Prophet gave him a measure in these things: for he says that he himself is the man of God, so that he may be seen to be near us who have God dwelling in us through the Holy Spirit: for he dwells in our hearts ours, and we are the temples of God. But it is hardly the same thing to say that the Word became man, and that God dwells in man; for although the words of the blessed Paul are true: For in him it pleased him to dwell all the fullness of the divinity corporeally (Colossians 2:8), that is, not שְׁפִיטָ; yet he says that there is one Father, and one Lord Jesus Christ, through whom all things are.

Let someone then say that Christ and the same spirit also dwell in man, and it is written about some: But they dwell in clay houses (Job. 4:19); of which we also are of the same clay: yet one is understood, and is by composition man from the flesh, and from the rational soul inhabiting the flesh. Why, then, does it not cease to disturb the correct and stable system of faith? For he just says one Christ, and the Son, and the Lord, and the same God and man at the same time: he just places him among the prophets, calling the man himself θεοφορον, not knowing that perhaps he is equal to himself, or to ourselves, if indeed he is not really God, but rather a temple. in whom the Word dwells, as also in us. It is true that these things are not to be so, divine Scripture has commanded: The Word was made flesh and dwelt among us (John 1:14); lest anyone should think that by conversion and exchange he himself was converted into the nature of the flesh. But he who became flesh, or man, is not a divine man, but rather God, who plunged himself into voluntary emptiness, and made his own flesh from a woman, and flesh not inanimate and without sense, but animated and rational.

But we remember that the temple also called him his body: for the rest he did not make an indwelling, as in us, by the spirit; but by union one is meant Christ, and the Son, and the Lord.

SIXTH ANATHEMA

Let him say that Christ is God or Lord, the Word of God the Father; and no more confesses the same God and man at the same time, because the Word was made flesh, according to the Scriptures; let him be.

CRIMINATION OF HERETICS.

Blessed Paul indeed calls that which has been assumed by the Word of God the form of a servant. But since there is an assumption before the union; But the blessed Paul, disputing about the assumption, called the form of a servant the assumed nature: therefore the name of slavery no longer has any place, having been united; for if the blessed Paul, writing to those who believed in him, said: Therefore he is no longer a servant, but a Son (Gal. 4:7); and the Lord further said to the disciples: I will no longer call you servants, but friends (John 15:15); much more the beginning of our nature, by which we also merited the grace of adoption, was freed by the appeal of servitude.

Therefore, we acknowledge God in the form of a servant, because of the form of God united to him, and we agree with the Prophet's calling the child Emmanuel, and the messenger of great counsel, and a miracle, and a counselor, and a strong and dominant God, and the prince of peace, and the father of the age to come (Isaiah 7, 14; 9:6). But the same prophet even after the gathering, preaching the assumed nature, calls that which is from the seed of Abraham a servant, thus saying: You are my servant, Israel, and I will glory in you (Is. 49:3); and again: Thus, saith the Lord, who formed me from the womb to be his servant (Ibid. 5). And a little later: Behold, I have given thee as a testament of the race to the light of the nations, that thou mayest be for salvation unto the ends of the earth (Isaiah 42:7; 49:6). Now that which was made in the womb is not God the Word, but the form of a servant: for God the Word was not turned into flesh but assumed flesh having a rational soul.

THE ORTHODOX RESPONSE

The mystery of the dispensation of the Only Begotten, which was made in the flesh, will make our discourses no less common now, and will very easily demonstrate that they are not held irrationally: for who is in the form of the only begotten Son of God and the Father, who is in all things equal to his begotten, who is of the same glory and freedom. taking the form of a servant, he was called the brother of those who bear the yoke of slavery, that is, ours. And so, as if one of us weighed the didragm with tax collectors, and became under the law as a man, who is a lawgiver as God; And then he taught his disciples that the Son is both in truth and in the form of a servant because of the flesh, and that by his nature he is a free man, since he is from God and is God. Nevertheless, having the proper form of a servant, because of the measure of emptiness, he weighed the tax on the tax collectors.

Therefore, even if someone says that he was called a servant by the voice of the prophets, no one should suffer offense in any way. Yet he did not throw away the measure of the most wise emptiness, taking a similar form for us who are under the yoke of slavery. Thus, also he calls God Himself the Father, since He Himself is God by nature and from the Father; and in no part is he inferior to the majesty of the Father.

Nestorius, therefore, writing thus of Christ: Therefore, he who suffered is the merciful pontiff, not God, the vivifier of him who suffered, naming the Word of Christ God, and adding these things: But he was both a child, and the Lord of children (Serm. 6, whether 6); We vehemently affirm that these words were spoken neither rightly nor competently, but impiously. For if the God of Christ is the Word of God and of the Father, it is absolutely necessary to be two, and beyond doubt. But in what way is the same thing to be understood, both the child and the child's Lord? Therefore, it is not to be said that God is his own, and the Lord Emmanuel, since he is the same, and God and man at the same time, as if the Word of God had been made and incarnated as man. Indeed, that divinity is one thing by its nature, and humanity another, no one can dispute: moreover, Christ is from both, from deity and humanity, according to the dispensational union.

SEVENTH ANATHEMA

If he calls Christ, as a man, helped by the operation of God's Word, and assigns to him the glory of the Only Begotten, as others besides him; let him be.

CRIMINATION OF HERETICS.

If the nature of man is mortal, and the Word of God, being life and life-giving, raised up the temple, which was dissolved by the Jews, and raised it to the heavens, how was the form of the servant not glorified by the form of God? For if any nature is mortal, it became immortal, because of the union of the Word and God, it received what it did not have; but taking what she had not, and being glorified, she was glorified by him who gave; for which reason the Apostle cries: According to the operation of the power of his power, which he operated in Christ, raising him from the dead (Eph. 1:20).

THE ORTHODOX RESPONSE

Those who name Christ do not designate to their hearers a common man like us, but a man made, and the incarnate Word of God. Therefore, even if it is said that he accomplished some wonderful and divine works through his body, which provided him with the office of instrument, nevertheless he himself is the one who works, Christ the Lord of the powers, and no one else provides the principality, so that he can work. just as he gave power to the blessed disciples to cast out unclean spirits, and to cure every disease and every infirmity in the people. Hence the blessed Paul said: For I dare not speak anything of those things which Christ has not accomplished through me, by word and deed, by the power of signs and wonders, by the power of the Holy Spirit (Rom. 15:18). Even the blessed disciples, rejoicing, sometimes approached Christ, saying: Lord, even the demons are subject to us in your name (Luke 10:17).

Helped by Christ in spirit we say saints, as if others besides him. Do we not, in the same way and with the same reason, understand Jesus himself, helped by the Word in the spirit, as if he were another Son besides the only begotten Son of God? For the unity itself shows us one thing, and we refuse to divide it into two: for though the Word was made flesh, according to the Scriptures, yet so is the only-begotten Son, according to the true union, which no one can grasp in the mind's thought.

Therefore, Christ Jesus is the only one, who through his body, as if through an instrument, worked the divine signs. Nor do we say that Christ himself was assisted by the operation, the example of the saints: for this is impious and greatly culpable. But if he raised his own body from the dead, as life himself, and the giver of life, he glorified it, showing that it was his own life-giving nature, but he did not give any other glory to anyone besides himself. Certainly, he said to the heavenly Father: Father, glorify me with the glory that I had before you before the world was made (John 17:5); although he was both God, and from God by nature, and the Lord of glory. In what way then, as if in need of the glory, which he had before the world, does he replace the glory? For after he became man, even through his flesh: the grace of God tasted death for all (Heb. 2:9), as the blessed Paul says. Refusing the reproach of the injury that arose from it, he foretells the resurrection, by which it is known that he is both life and life-giving, as God, and in that way also he is believed by us.

He therefore glorified no one else, but himself, designating the temple truly joined to himself stronger than death; but we believe that the body, which is united to itself, is not empty, nor without sense and mind.

THE EIGHTH ANATHEMA.

If he dares to say that it is necessary for the assumed man to be co-worshipped with God the Word, and to be glorified, and to conjure up God, as one with another; and no more does he worship Emmanuel with one veneration, and assigns to him one glorification, because the Word was made flesh (John 1:14); let him be.

CRIMINATION OF HERETICS.

Indeed, as I have often said, we offer one glorification to the Lord Christ, and we acknowledge the same God and man at the same time: for this reason of unification has taught us, but we will not refuse to say the properties of nature. For neither was God the Word turned into flesh; nor again did man lose what he had been and was transformed into the nature of God; therefore, saying the property of both natures, we worship Christ the Lord.

THE ORTHODOX RESPONSE

But we who are accustomed to perceive better and more truths, and treat finer senses for a more certain and correct interpretation of mysteries, according to the precepts of the sacred letters, and according to the custom of the holy Fathers, we do not say a man assumed by God the Word, and conjoined to him, to be understood externally through σχέσιν; but rather we define man as being himself. For this reason, those who dare to say that man was assumed, we lead to be outside the bounds of the dogmas of piety, which affirm that he ought to be worshiped together with the Son of God, as one with another: for if God is the same, and man at the same time, he is worshiped more as one. by one adoration, and not co-worshipped and conjoined with God, lest it be believed that he was simply a common man, and like our Emmanuel, made a partaker of the divine glory by the benefit of it.

NINTH ANATHEMA

Let him say that Jesus Christ is one Lord, glorified by the Spirit by his own power, as if by another's power, and receive from him, that he may work against unclean spirits, and fulfill the divine signs, and no longer be his own spirit, through which he worked the divine signs; let him be.

CRIMINATION OF HERETICS.

Here clearly not only those who observe piety in this world, but also those who were before, preachers of the truth, and the writers of the divine Gospels themselves, and the chorus of the holy apostles; moreover, he also ventured to anathematize the archangel Gabriel. For according to the flesh Christ was made of the Holy Spirit, he was the first, and before Mary's conception he foretold; and after the conception Joseph taught, even asking Mary: How will this be for me, since I do not know a man (Luke 1, 35)? saying: The Holy Spirit will come upon you, and the power of the Most High will overshadow you; therefore, because he is born holy, he will be called the Son of God. But to Joseph: Do not be afraid to take Mary as your spouse, for what was born in her is from the Holy Spirit (Matthew 1:20). And the Evangelist: And when Mary Joseph, his mother, was betrothed, he said, she was found in the womb having the Holy Spirit (Ibid., 18). And the Lord himself also entered the synagogue of the Jews, when he had received the prophet Isaiah, and had read that passage in which he says: The Spirit of the Lord is upon me, for whose sake he anointed me (Luke 4:18); and what follows, he added: Today this scripture has been fulfilled in your ears (Ibid., 21). And the blessed Peter, when speaking to the Jews, said: Jesus of Nazareth, whom God anointed with the Holy Spirit (Acts 10:38); and Isaiah sang many centuries ago: A rod shall come out of the root of Jesse, and a flower shall come up from his root, and the spirit of God shall rest upon him, the spirit of wisdom and understanding, the spirit of counsel and power, the spirit of knowledge and piety; the spirit of the fear of God will fill him (Isaiah 11:1). And again: Behold my son whom I have loved; my beloved, in whom my soul rested. I will put my spirit upon him, and he will announce judgment to the nations (Matthew 12:18). And the Evangelist also set forth this testimony in his writings; and the Lord himself said in the Gospels to the Jews: But if by the Spirit of God I cast out demons, surely the kingdom of God has come upon you (Luke 11:20). And John said: He who sent me to baptize in water, he himself said to me: On whom you see the Spirit descending and remaining on him, he is the one who baptizes in the Holy Spirit (John 1:33).

Therefore, that most diligent examiner of divine dogmas did not anathematize the prophets alone, and the apostles, nor only the archangel Gabriel; but he also extends blasphemy against the very Savior of all. For we showed Christ himself, indeed, only to the Jews, after he had recited: The Spirit of the Lord is upon me, because he anointed me; said: Today this scripture has been fulfilled in your ears (Luke 4:18); just to those who had said that he casts out demons through Beelzebub, he said that he casts out demons in the spirit of God (Luke 11:20).

But we do not call God the Word formed by the Holy Spirit, and anointed, which is of the same substance with the Spirit, and coeternal; but the human nature, which was assumed by him in the last times.

But the proper spirit of the Son, if, because it is of the same nature, and proceeds from the Father, he said, we will consent, and we will receive the pious voice; But if it has its existence from the Son, or through the Son, then we will cast out blasphemy and impiety. For we believe in the Lord saying: The Spirit that proceeds from the Father (John 15:26); to the divine Paul who also said: But we have not received the spirit of the world, but the spirit which is from the Father (1 Cor. 2:12).

THE ORTHODOX RESPONSE

I have already said before that the force of the chapters is opposed to Nestorius's vanities, nay, to his blasphemies, and to his vehemently impolite sayings. For when he said of the Holy Spirit (Serm. 2): He who bestowed so much glory on Christ, who made him terrible to the demons, who gave him his assumption into the heavens; and of Christ, as of some common man like us, by babbling these things, he necessarily became anathematized. Not in those who say that Jesus was glorified by the Holy Spirit, that is, the Word of God made man; but more on those who impudently mention that he himself was used by the power of the Holy Spirit, as if it were something else. For we remember him clearly saying of the Holy Spirit: He will glorify me (John 18:14). We know, moreover, that by the operation of the Holy Spirit he will crush unclean and evil spirits.

But we do not say that any one of the prophets was himself used by the power of the Holy Spirit, as if it were alien: for it was his, and is, the Holy Spirit, as well as the Father's. And this the divine Paul pointed out to us most clearly, writing thus: But those who are in the flesh cannot please God; but you are not in the flesh, but in the spirit, if indeed the spirit of God dwells in you. But if anyone does not have the Spirit of Christ, this is not his (Rom. 4:9). For the Holy Spirit proceeds from God and the Father, according to the voice of the

Savior, but is not alien to the Son: for he has all things with the Father. And he himself shows this about the Holy Spirit: All that the Father has is mine, therefore I said to you that he will receive from me and will announce it to you (John 16:15). The Holy Spirit therefore glorified Jesus, working miracles; nevertheless, as his own spirit, he is neither better by another's power, nor better by himself, by what is meant by God.

Therefore, we did not blaspheme against the holy angels, nor against the prophets, as he dared to say, who only learned to curse. True, since it is still intended for him, and for those like him, to divide the one Christ into two; namely, on him who is glorified, and on him who helps the operation: they unwisely criticize every reason of piety which can bring them back from such a wrong opinion.

Finally, the accuser, making mention of the blessed Gabriel: He who said that Christ was made according to the flesh from the Holy Spirit, he was the first and before the conception foretold. Christ is therefore another, who according to the flesh; and another specially Christ, who is the Word from God the Father. Where then is the union? And what will be the profit from this, if there are two Christs, and each is understood and called separately?

Let them, then, feign a face and a person of piety, say one Christ, yet let them who believe two hear from us: How long will you limp with both feet (3 Kings 18:21)? For it is better to follow the right steps, keeping the right faith and being steadfast, and not being swayed by foolish thoughts.

THE TENTH ANATHEMA

The divine Scripture mentions that Christ became the pontiff and apostle of our confession. For he offered himself for us as an aroma of sweetness to God and the Father. If, then, someone says that our pontiff and apostle were made, not the Word of God itself, then, of course, when he was made flesh, and man next to us; but as another, apart from himself, separate man from the woman:

or if someone says that he offered the offering himself for himself, and no more only for us, for he did not make a sacrifice who knew no sin; let him be.

CRIMINATION OF HERETICS.

The unconvertible nature was not converted into the nature of the flesh; but he assumed a human nature, and appointed it over the common priests, as the blessed Paul teaches, saying: For every pontiff, taken from among men, is appointed for men in those things which belong to God, that he may offer gifts and sacrifices for sins, that he may forgive those who do not know, and they err. Since he himself is also surrounded by infirmity, therefore he must offer for sins, just as for the people, so also for himself (Heb. 5:1). And soon explaining this very thing: As Aaron, so also Christ (Ibid., 5). Then, showing the weakness of the assumed nature, he says: He who, in the days of his flesh, offered prayers and supplications to him who is able to save him from death, with loud cries and tears, was heard for mercy. And indeed, when he was the Son, he learned obedience from those who suffered, and became perfect for all who obey him for the sake of eternal salvation, called by God a high priest according to the order of Melchizedek (Ibid., 7).

Who, then, was perfected by the labors of virtue, when he was not perfect by nature? Who is it that has learned obedience by experiments, which he did not know before the experiment? Who is it that lived with reverence? Who with loud cries and tears offering supplications, and not being able to save himself, but beseeching Him who is able to save, and seeking deliverance from death? Not God the Word, immortal, impassive, incorporeal: Whose remembrance, according to the Prophet, is rejoicing, and relief from tears for he will wipe away every tear from every face (Isa. 25, 9, sec. 70). And again the Prophet: I was mindful, says he, of God (Ps. 76, 4), and I rejoiced that he crowns the illustrious with piety (Dan. 13, 2); that everything belongs to the Father (John 16:15); which is a very similar image of the parent (Colossians 1:15, 39); that he showed the Father in himself (John 14:10): but more, that he had been taken from the seed of David by God, mortal and susceptible; which fed him to death, although afterwards he himself destroyed the dominion of death, because of the divinity of the one who assumed it; that he walked in all righteousness; what he said to John: Without a way, it behooves us to fulfill all righteousness (Matthew 3:15); that the pontificate received an appellation according to the order of Melchizedek (Heb. 5:10): for he himself bore the infirmity of nature, and not the almighty God the Word. For this reason, the blessed Paul had said before: For we have not a pontiff who cannot sympathize with our infirmities; but having been tempted in all things to likeness without sin (Heb. 4:15).

Almost all of this περικοπὴ is read in the 5th synod. Indeed, Theodoretus and Cyril contend in this place with great force of arguments, but with greater zeal of the parties: for what is being dealt with, as I have more than once pointed out, is the case of Proclus, whom Theodoretus hated, as a noble adversary of Nestorius; Cyril, as the leader of those who fought for the faith of Constantinople, had a good reputation. Cyril objects to the conversion of the Word into flesh by Theodoret; Cyril, on the other hand, reproaches the lamentable insanity, the ignorance of the mystery in question, the assertion of ἐνόσεως σεφιτιῆς, agreement with Nestorius, impiety and contradiction. All this speech of Cyril can fix a great cross on the patron Theodoret.

But that nature, which was taken from us for us, has experienced our passions without sin; not who assumed it for our salvation. And at the beginning of this chapter, he teaches again: Consider the apostle and pontiff of our confession, Jesus, faithful to him who made him, just as Moses was in all his house (Heb. 3:1). But whoever, thinking rightly, would ever say that he was God the Word, uncreated and coeternal with the Father; but him who was of the seed of David, who, free from all sin, was our pontiff, offering himself as a victim to God for us, having certainly in himself the Word of God united to himself and inseparably conjoined?

THE ORTHODOX RESPONSE

When Israel had offended God and provoked him to anger, the prophet Jeremiah said in sorrow: Who will give water to my head and a fountain of tears to my eyes, so that I may wipe out these people day and night (Jeremiah 9:1)?

And I think that voices of this kind are not more fitting for Israel than for those who always have a clear and open mouth for Christ: Who also brings down the ineffable glory, daring, and arrogant (2 Pet. 2, 10), according to what is written. But they are the most deserving of weeping and lamentation, who, in their infinite madness, neglecting the straight and blameless path of piety to Christ, follow a crooked orbit and detours, and defile the beauty of the truth with the wrong inventions of their thoughts.

Therefore, let those who feel hated by all, wandering in the knowledge of the Scriptures, ignorant of the great and venerable mystery of the Incarnation, listen. They affirm that he became flesh, that is, man; not by conversion, or by exchange, but by the power of mysterious unification, and therefore we say one thing, Jesus Christ the Lord, and one faith, and one holy baptism.

These, however, are averse from the correct dogmas, and oppose a harsh and unusual sense against the sacred letters; They look only to that which seems to be good for them, and they mention the man assumed by the Word of God, perhaps according to what was said by one of the prophets: I was not a prophet, nor the son of a prophet; but I was a shepherd plucking sycamores; and God took me from the sheep (Amos 7:14); or perhaps, as the blessed David said: The Lord accepts the meek (Psal. 146, 6); according to σχέσιν, that is, and spiritual familiarity, which by will, and grace, and sanctification, we ourselves also have: for adhering to the Lord, we are one spirit, according to what is written (1 Cor. 6:17). But this by no means means that God was made man; nor that he, in the same way as we, partook of flesh and blood, but rather that he assumed man, in no other covenant than that by which it is said that he assumed both the apostles and the prophets and all the other saints.

Does the divine Paul deceive those who are sanctified by faith, clearly saying of the Only Begotten, that when he was rich, he became poor (II Cor. 8:9)? Far from it: for the greatest preacher of truth will never lie. But who is rich, and how he became poor, let us now also examine more carefully. Indeed, if, as they trust to say and feel, man is assumed by God; How did he who was accepted by God become poor, when he was enlightened by the higher dignities of his nature? for he was glorified. But if this is not true, the assumption will be criticized by them, since it has brought down to a lower and more inglorious mode of humanity. It's really stupid to feel that way. Therefore he who was taken up was not made poor; It remains, then, that we may say that God the Word, when he was rich, became our poor.

But how did he become poor? Now, as it is necessary, let us pay attention: indeed, it is unconvertible by nature, without doubt, nor has it abandoned itself, passed into the nature of the flesh; for that which remained, that is, God. Where then shall we see the humility of poverty? In the age that God assumed one like ours, as Nestorius' impiety parasites dared to say? And what should be the measure of poverty and emptiness? At the same time, perhaps he wanted to honor someone like us? But by no agreement granting benefits, the Almighty God is violated: how then was he made poor? Because God was by nature, and the Son of God and the Father, man was made of the seed of David; He was born according to the flesh, and underwent a servile measure, that is, a human one, who is the maker of all things: for, having become man, He is not ashamed to undergo the measure of humanity. For he who did not refuse to be like us, how could he refuse those things by which a man could show that he truly became like us? If, therefore, we remove him from men, from things, and from words, we are in no way different from those who, if it were possible, would rob him even with their own flesh, who do not believe in the divine Scriptures, completely overthrowing the mystery of the Incarnation, the salvation of the world, hope, faith, and resurrection.

Let someone say that it is little proper to God the Word, and in no way fitting, to weep, to fear death, to refuse the cup, to undergo the office of a priest. I, too, very willingly agree that these things do not in the least agree with divine nature and glory. Nevertheless, in these I see poverty, which he willingly endured for our sake. If the insults of emptiness seem heavy to you, all the more wonder at the Son's charity towards us; for what you say is so indecent, and so small, God has made this for your sake lovable to himself.

He shed tears after the manner of men, so that he himself should restrain your tears. He escaped dispensationally, allowing the flesh to suffer sometimes, which is his own, so that we might be made the most confident. He refused the cup, that the cross might accuse the Jews of impiety. He is said to be infirm according to humanity, in order to deliver you from your infirmities. He offered prayers and supplications, that he might also lend an easy ear to your supplications, that you might learn not to sleep in temptations, but to concentrate your mind more on prayers. And therefore he accused the holy apostles of sleeping, saying: Thus could you not watch with me for one hour? watch and pray, lest you enter into temptation (Matthew 26:4). For by offering himself as a reformation of a happy life, he profited the world; therefore he made familiar the infirmities of humanity, so that it might be believed that he had truly become man, when he nevertheless remained what he was, that is, God.

But I do not know how those who pretend to say that Christ is one, and Son, and Lord, and the same God and man at the same time, say that the Word of God was not called the pontiff and the apostle of our confession, when he became man; but they affirm that another, I do not know who, a separate man himself, who was of the seed of David, was called to this; For he said in this way (Serm. 6, which is the third in Proclus): He who is faithful to God has become a priest; for he was made, and had not always been; here, who gradually advanced, heretical, to the dignity of the priests. Then, as he thinks, desiring to confirm the truth of his words, he says: About which Luke also cried in the Gospels: But Jesus was advancing in age, wisdom, and grace. And again: But since this is the only pontiff who sympathizes with us, and is related, and certain, do not be misled by his nature: for he was sent to us out of the promised blessing and the seed of Abraham, bringing with him a bodily sacrifice for himself and his kind.

But the best rival of that madness, the good man Theodoret, is not ashamed to say: He assumed a human nature and ordained it over the common priests, just as Paul also says: For every pontiff taken from among men is appointed for men in those things which belong to God, who is able to sympathize to those who are ignorant and err, since he himself is surrounded by infirmity; and therefore he ought, as for the people, so also for himself to offer for sins. Did not Emmanuel make us a common man, as far as he is concerned? Aren't these, mentioned above, also genuine opinions, giving birth to the same blasphemy? What do you say? Fear the mode of priesthood in Christ the Savior of all; nor does it seem appropriate to minister to God the Word in a human manner, because of the dispensation? Uncover your face, a person who has been laid down, and openly deny the incarnation of the Word of God, for which reason he was also named pontiff. Do you see him immolating himself, like others and to the greater God, the Father? Have you contemplated offering sacrifices, the example of those who are accepted by men, and who can sympathize with the ignorant and erring, because they too are in our infirmities? Have you not considered that the faith of all, or the confession of faith, consecrates both to the Holy Spirit and to the Father? Is this the way of human ministry to ask for faith from those who have been offered a fragrance of sweetness in the spirit? Observe how differently, when God is, though in human fashion, he is said to minister because of the dispensation: for he sits with God and the Father, and is seen in high places. Does that of humanity terrify you, nor does that of divinity deliver you from fear? You do not admit, judging from the facts themselves, that God is at the same time Emmanuel the man; but so impudently and inconsiderately, nay, running beyond the bounds of all impiety, you say that he himself was accomplished by labors and valor, and that he advanced little by little to the dignity of a pontiff. If he prospered, where was the emptiness, and where did he become poor? If it is completed by virtue, it is certainly imperfect, and in time it becomes perfect. But whatever is not perfect in virtue is contained in fault and vice; and that which is contained in vice is in sin. How then is it written of him that he committed no sin (1 Peter 2:22)?

He ventured to say what is written below: Who then became a priest? Who is perfect in virtue, when he is not perfect in nature? Who has learned obedience through temptations, which he did not know before temptations? Who has lived with reverence, and with strong crying and tears, and offering supplications, when he could not save himself, but imploring him who could save him? O boldest and most wicked voice! What tears of such impious believers will be able to wipe away the sins? If you agree to the union, how did you not know what you say about God, who became man? He humbled himself for your sake, and you impiously cry out: Be merciful, Lord, this will never happen to you. Therefore, you will hear him say: Get behind me, Satan; you are a stumbling block to me (Matthew 16:22).

But in the conclusion of what he said, he said: Therefore, he who is of the seed of David is a priest, having in himself, that is, the Word of God united to himself, and inseparably conjoined. And how is he united to the Word of God that which is of the seed of David, if he has appointed the priesthood to him alone, who is of the seed of David? For if the union is true, there are not two at all, but one, and only one, who is understood to be Christ from both.

It is certain, then, that they pretend to confess a union, inciting the hearts of the simple: for they believe that conjunction is σεφιτὴν, and that it was made from without, which we also had, when we become partakers of the divine nature itself through the spirit. Therefore, we must not adhere to their vanities, but to the correct and blameless faith, and to the evangelical and apostolic sanctions.

THE ELEVENTH ANATHEMA.

Let it not be confessed that the flesh of the Lord is alive, and that it is proper to the Word of God himself, but that it is that of any other, joined indeed by dignity, or by indwelling alone; and I will no more vivify, as I said before, because it is proper to the Word, which is able to vivify all things; let him be.

CRIMINATION OF HERETICS.

As far as it appears, he strives for obscurity, in order to hide his impiety, who feels the same as the heretics; but nothing is more powerful than the truth, which can reveal the darkness with its rays of lies. Let us make his faith ἑτερόδοξον, enlightened, manifest. In the first place, indeed, he never mentions the rational flesh, nor is the perfect man, who was assumed, confessed; but everywhere he says flesh, following the dogmas of Apollinaris. Then, expressing the opinion of the mixture in other voices, he sprinkles it with words, for hence he clearly says that the flesh of the Lord is inanimate, when he says: If anyone confesses that the flesh of the Lord is not proper to the Word of God himself, but that it belongs to someone else besides himself, let him be anathema. Hence it appears that he did not confess that God the Word assumed a soul, but only flesh; but the very being of the flesh is for the soul: but we say the living, animated, and reasonable flesh of the Lord, because of the vivifying deity united to himself.

But he also confesses, though unwillingly, the difference of natures, naming flesh and God the Word, and saying that it was his own flesh: therefore, God the Word was not converted into the nature of flesh; but it has its own flesh, that is, the assumed nature, and it has made it alive by union.

THE ORTHODOX RESPONSE.

Those who have slipped away from right and true thoughts through incompetence, almost even say: We have placed our hope in a lie, and we will be covered with a lie (Isaiah 28:15). For on whomsoever it pleases them, they utter a judgment without consideration; nor do they remember the divine Scriptures which say: Judge righteous judgment (Zech. 7:9). And again: A false witness will not go unpunished (Prov. 19:5). For we say that the holy body of Christ, the savior of all, is life-giving. For it is not simply like our man, but common; but the more truly proper property of the Word, which gives life to all things. But the proper way is so that each one of us may be said to have his own body.

This handsome man, however, did not exceed the limits of his talkativeness aimed at us, although he agreed with what we said. He insinuates upon us again the infamy of Apollinaris's impiety; nor is he ashamed, reminding me of other words and sayings, to conceal the matter of mixture or confusion, and to call inanimate flesh joined to the Word. But perhaps someone will say to him: O most excellent man, you will also accuse blessed John of the same crimes; for he says: The Word was made flesh (John 1:14). Come, then, with him even insolently, and say that the soul does not remember him as rational, but to call the Lord's inanimate flesh. What if you heard Christ, the Savior of all, say: Verily I say unto you, except ye eat the flesh of the Son of man, and drink his blood, ye shall not have life in you. And again: He that eateth my flesh, and drinketh my blood, abideth in me, and I in him. And again: But the bread that I will give is my flesh for the life of the world (John 6:54). An insult, if it will be seen, even to the Word itself: for it mentions only the flesh and does not make any mention of the rational soul in these things.

But you, if you were shrewd and wise, would not be ignorant of the fact that generally even by the mere mention of flesh an animal, which consists of soul and body, is designated, that is, man. For it is written that all flesh shall see the salvation of God (Isaiah 40:5). Therefore, he who says that the Word was made flesh is not entirely ignorant of the fact that he also makes reasonable mention of the soul. It is true, as I said at the beginning, that failing in his proofs, he finds for himself a lie under cover, and tries to slander himself, that he may seem to say something.

But truly, that man was assumed by God, it does not seem to the holy Fathers: for they never believed so; but rather they said that God the Word became man, and was united to flesh, having a rational soul. But the union is unconfused, and without conversion at all: for the Word of God is unconvertible, and so we believe.

TWELFTH ANATHEMA.

Let him not confess that the Word of God suffered in the flesh, and was crucified in the flesh, and tasted death in the flesh, and became the first-born from the dead, because, as God, he gives life, and is life-giving; let him be.

CRIMINATION OF HERETICS.

Passions are characteristic of a susceptible nature; impassive, superior to passions; The form of the servant therefore suffered, adhering to himself, that is, also the form of God, and indeed permitting him to suffer, for the sake of the salvation which had been brought about from his sufferings. but his sufferings, for the sake of union, saying: therefore, it was not God who suffered, but man, who was taken from us by God. That is why the blessed Isaiah, foretelling before, cries out: A man in a plague, and knowing how to bear infirmity (Isaiah

53:3). And the Lord Christ himself said to the Jews: Why do you want me to kill a man who has told you the truth (John 8:40)? It is not life itself that is killed, but he who has a mortal nature. And the Lord, teaching this elsewhere, said to the Jews: Take down that temple, and in three days I will rebuild it. Therefore, he who is of David is indeed freed; but he resurrected the freed, only-begotten Word of God, who was impassibly born of the Father centuries ago.

THE ORTHODOX RESPONSE

Indeed, the nature of the Word is unquestionably impassive, and this, I think, is uncertain to any man. For no one should fall into such insane madness as to say that our infirmities hold that mysterious and superior nature to the passions. But since the passion was to save the world; But it was impossible for the Word God to suffer anything in his nature; He underwent the dispensation wisely: for he made his own body what he could suffer, so that he himself may be said to have suffered with a patient body, although he himself by his nature remained impassive.

True, since he willingly suffered in the flesh, therefore he is and is called the Savior of all. For as Paul says: The grace of God tasted death for all (Heb. 2:9). Indeed, even the divine Peter testifies very wisely, saying: I therefore suffer Christ for us (1 Pet. 4, 1). Certainly not in the nature of the deity, but in the flesh. Finally, in what way is the Lord of glory said to have been crucified? In what way, too, by whom and in whom all things are ordered (1 Cor. 2:8; Heb. 2:10), as the blessed Paul says, was given by God and the Father the head of the body of the Church, becoming the firstborn from the dead? that is to say, he suffered familiarly the passions of the flesh; But the Lord of glory was by no means a man similar and common to us.

But perhaps you will say that unity is sufficient to prove that Christ and the crucified Lord are one. Therefore, let all things be said to be his, and let it be believed that the Word of God is the Savior, indeed permanent and impassive according to the nature of the deity, but suffering in the flesh, according to what Peter said: for his was his own body through true union, which tasted death. Finally, how from the Jews according to the flesh Christ and God over all, and blessed forever, amen (Rom. 9:18). In whose death are we baptized? By confessing whose resurrection are we justified? Or any common man? Or, what is more true, do we announce the death of the man of God who became man and suffered for us in the flesh, and confessing the resurrection, do we lay off the burden of sins? For we are bought with a price, not corruptible with silver or gold; but with the precious blood, like the pure and spotless lamb of Christ (1 Cor. 6:20; 1 Pet. 1:19).

Indeed, it is not difficult to mention many more and other things above these, and to set forth the examples of the holy Fathers; for it is written: Give a wise man an opportunity, and he will be wiser; announce to the just, and he will add to be perceived (Prov. 9:9).

These words: 'the willing has suffered', πέπονθεν ἑκών, Eutherius expounded in his speech just as these: 'the word has suffered in the flesh', ἔπαθεν ὁ Θεὸς Λόγος σαρκί. Furthermore, there is so much between Eranistus and the criticisms of the chapters, whether the affinity of the sentences, or the similarity of the words, that they do not so much show the same author, whom no one recognizes; but the same adversary also, whom few notice to be Cyril, which we shall show, I think, in the bulk of the works of Theodoret, which we are preparing, we shall soon, if it be God's will, submit to the press; , the judgment of the individual works will be established in such a way that several parts of which Mercator gave are proved to be wanting in the Sirmondian edition, and the history of each one, that is, the time, the causes, and the quality, will be told.

LATIN TEXT

Cyrillus reverendissimo et dilectissimo fratri, et consacerdoti Evoptio, in Domino salutem.

Legi quae a tua sanctimonia dudum mihi transmissa sunt, et affectum miratus sum, atque sinceritatem charitatis in Christo; oportere autem arbitror, nunc quoque attemperatissime exclamare, quod in libro Proverbiorum scriptum est: Frater a fratre adjutus, ut civitas bene munita (Prov. XVIII, 19). Et mihi quidem videtur charitas divinae Scripturae maxime fuisse laudibus honorata, et id recte, quippe cum habeat in se plenitudinem legis (Rom. XIII, 10), et virtutibus sit aliis praeferenda, ac sanctorum animis videatur esse mirabilis; nempe quam dicimus, non nudis, nec solis impleri verborum vocabulis, sed quae a rebus ipsis testimonium habeant. Quemadmodum enim pretiosissimi lapides, quos Indicos aiunt esse, non si quis de ipsorum pulchritudine commemoret, sed ipsi pulchri si fuerint, spectantium oculis admirandi sunt; ita ex ipsis exemplis praeclarum charitatis decus apparet bonis omnibus comparatum.

Hanc reverentia tua plurimi facit, sanctorum solita semper observare vestigia, et probatissimae vitae illorum laudes sectari. Accepi igitur, ut tuae sanctitatis affectum nunc quoque cognoscerem, tomum transmissum, quem composuisse dicitur contra anathematismos Theodoretus Cyri: ita enim oppidum illud audio nominari. Quo perlecto egi gratias maximas Deo, et illud dicere non cessavi: Domine, libera animam meam a labiis injustis, et a lingua dolosa (Psal. CXIX, 2).

Comperi enim ubique et in singulis capitulis mihi calumnias importari. Miratus igitur sum, virum non alienum a litteris, ut quidam de eo retulerunt, et sacrarum forte litterarum non mediocri scientia praeditum, in tantum ignorasse vim capitulorum, ut orta sit mihi suspicio, eum alienis desideriis ficta ignorantia fuisse gratificatum; ne scilicet videatur temere nobis, et sine aliquo colore detrahere: cum praesertim nihil prorsus arduum sit, nihil obscurum in nostris dictis, nisi me fallit opinio, nihil quod sit intellectu difficile. Verum quando necesse fuit, quamvis jam super his antea scripserimus, paucis ad eum quoque respondere, ne quis nos credat reticuisse convictos, aggrediar ad responsionem, quantum res patietur, brevitate servata.

Decuerat quidem ipsum maxime, cum Scripturarum habeat scientiam divinarum, volentem nobiscum de sacris mysteriis disputare, sacrarum tantummodo litterarum fecisse mentionem, ac non curiosas fabulas sordidasque proferre: meos etenim sermones MALO DISCORDIAE assimulare dignatur, et hanc fortasse probationem suae putat esse doctrinae. Unde et nos hanc ipsius nimiam sumus admirati scientiam: apparet enim illum propter profundam scilicet ingentemque doctrinam, MALUM non ignorasse DISCORDIAE; nec Paridem filium Priami.

Nam in epistola post alia: Praeterea non solum ipse haec ista asseruit; verum etiam nolentes ejus obtemperare blasphemiis anathematizare ausus est. Si tamen ipsius sunt ista inventa, ac non magis quidam inimicus veritati tamquam ex illo conscripta projecit in medium, sicut illud, quod in fabulis est, MALUM DISCORDIAE, quod flammam accendat.

Verum, nos his interim missis, proposito insistamus.

ANATHEMATISMUS PRIMUS.

Siquis non confiteatur Deum esse vere Emmanuel, et propterea sanctam Virginem esse Θεοτόκον: peperit enim carnaliter carnem factum Dei Verbum; anathema sit.

REPREHENSIO HAERETICI.

At nos, qui evangelicam traditionem sequimur, non carnem natura factum, et in carnem conversum Deum dicimus Verbum; invertibilis etenim et incommutabilis est Deus, de quo etiam David Propheta dicit: Tu autem idem es, et anni tui non deficient (Psal. CI, 28). Quod Paulus veritatis praedicator maximus de Filio dictum esse, in epistola ad Hebraeos asseruit (Heb. I, 11); et alibi per Prophetam Deus dicit: Ego sum, ego sum, et non commutatus sum (Malach. III, 6). Ergo si inconvertibilis et incommutabilis est Deus, conversionem et commutationem pati non potest; et si impossibile est, ut invertibilis convertatur, non est factum caro Deus Verbum conversum, sed assumpsit carnem, et habitavit in nobis juxta Evangeliorum voces. Et ipse id explanans Paulus divinus in epistola ad Philippenses ait: Hoc sentite in vobis, quod et in Christo Filio, qui cum in forma Dei esset, non rapinam arbitratus est, ut esset aequalis Deo, sed se exinanivit, formam servi accipiens (Philip. II, 5).

Apparet igitur ex dictis, quod Dei forma non sit in servi formam conversa; sed quod manens id quod erat, servi formam accepit. Ergo si non est factum caro Deus Verbum, sed carnem vivam et rationabilem assumpsit, non ipse natura ex Virgine natus est, conceptus, et fictus, et formatus, et inde initium, ut esset, accipiens, qui ante saecula est, et Deus, et apud Deum semper, et Patri adhaerens, et cum Patre cognoscendus adorandusque, cum sibi templum finxisset in utero virginali, adhaerebat ficto, et concepto, et formato, et nato. Qua de causa etiam Virginem sanctam Θεοτόκον vocamus, non quod Deum pepererit natura, sed quod hominem ediderit conjunctum Deo, qui ipsum formaverat.

Totus hic paragraphus refertur in V synodo, inter ea Theodoreti, adversus sanctum Cyrillum, quae anathemate damnata sunt; flagitium vero ipsius est, quod sancto Cyrillo contradicat in ea parte, in qua fidei ratio posita erat, nempe quod beata Virgo Verbum carnem factum pepererit, et non tantum hominem conjunctum Deo.

At si non est homo, qui in utero Virginis fictus est, sed Deus Verbum, qui est ante saecula; factura ergo sancti Spiritus est Deus Verbum. Nam quod in ea natum, est, inquit Gabriel, ex Spiritu sancto est (Matth. I, 20). At si increatum est unigenitum Dei Verbum, et ejusdem cum Patre substantiae, non est Spiritus sancti factura. Si autem non Deum Verbum in utero Virginis Spiritus formavit, superest, ut servi formam intelligamus et formatam et fictam esse natura.

Sed quoniam non tantum erat servi forma, sed templum habitatorem habens Deum Verbum, juxta Pauli vocem: Quoniam in ipso, inquit, complacuit omnem plenitudinem deitatis habitare corporaliter (Coloss. I, 19); non tantum ἀνθρωποτόκον, sed et Θεοτόκον sanctam Virginem vocamus; ἀντρωποτόκον, propter fictionem et formationem; Θεοτόκον, propter ἕνωσιν, appellantes: ideoque puer, qui natus est, Emmanuel est vocatus; nec Deus ab humana natura separatus, nec homo deitate nudus. Emmanuel enim significat, nobiscum esse Deum, juxta Evangeliorum voces; nobiscum autem Deus, et eum significat, qui ex nobis pro nobis assumptus est, et Deum Verbum, quod assumpsit, ostendit. Ergo Emmanuel puer propter Deum, qui assumpsit; et Virgo Θεοτόκος propter conjunctionem Dei formae servi; neque in carnem Deus Verbum conversus est: sed Dei forma servi formam accepit.

RESPONSIO ORTHODOXI.

Plurimum et saepe incusavimus eos qui recusant confiteri Deum esse vere Emmanuel, et sanctam Virginem esse Θεοτόκον, ideo quod peperit secundum carnem Dei Verbum, tunc cum est factum caro, id est, homo. At vero is, qui tam recte dicta a nobis accusat, si Deum vere esse nescit Emmanuel; si non est natum carnaliter ex sacra Virgine caro factum Dei Verbum, juxta Scripturas; cur non magis palam clamabat: Quid agis, vir bone? Eructas infandos sermones, dogmata obteris veritatis. Non est Deus vere Emmanuel, nec Virgo sancta Θεοτόκος, ut etiam nos haec ita clamitanti, dicentique, ea quae a divina Scriptura dicta sunt, sapienter opponentes, et apostolicae atque evangelicae fidei traditionem, et sanctorum Patrum confessionem, qui suo tempore Nicaeae congregati sunt, proferentes, persuaderemus, quod neque recte, neque honeste dicta nostra conetur arguere; immo magis divinae Scripturae reluctari festinet.

Sed prudens argutusque tractator, illis, quae eum oportuerat et necesse fuerat dicere, praetermissis, et cum nihil horum tetigisset, omnino in aliam se contulit viam: dicere enim aggressus est statim, quod Dei Verbum sit conversione validius, et quod non in naturam carnis transformatum sit, tamquam si hoc verum, esse anathematismus vel sentiat, vel affirmet.

Audiat igitur hic, qui orationi alterius nescit occurrere: sermones, homo, sine causa vanos exerces, et reluctaris opinioni vel nobis invisae. Novimus enim nos quoque, quod nec umbram quidem conversionis divina illa excellensque natura perpetiatur, et quod Dei Verbum in naturam non commigraverit carnis, deitate deposita.

Verum quando a Dei forma servi formam assumptam esse commemorat, doceat nos, sine substantiis solae et per se ipsae inter se formae convenerint. At id, opinor, ipse quoque non ita esse confitebitur: neque enim species tantum sine substantiis, et formae inter se per ἕνωσιν dispensatoriam convenerunt; sed rerum ipsarum sive substantiarum conventus est factus, ut inhumanationis ratio vere facta esse credatur. Ergo etsi Dei Verbum carnem factum esse dicamus, non tamen confusionem, nec commixtionem, nec rursus conversionem, aut commutationem ei dicimus contigisse; sed ipsum conjunctum esse, arcana ineffabilique ratione, corpori sancto habenti animam rationabilem: quidquid enim adunari dicitur, non confunditur, sed aliud sibi magis assumit.

Affirmamus igitur, Dei Patris Verbum assumpsisse sibi sanctam et animatam carnem, et esse vere inconfuseque, ex ipsa vulva, conjunctum, exiisse quidem hominem, Deum tamen verum sic quoque remansisse; ideo et Virgo sancta Θεοτόκος est. Supervacuum autem esse opinor, eam etiam ἀνθρωποτόκον vocari. Nam si essent quidam adeo mente capti, ut dicerent, naturam Verbi ex carne, tamquam fontem suae originis habuisse, et suae exstantiae inde initium fuisse sortitum, fortasse non absque aliqua ratione facere viderentur, qui eam ἀνθρωποτόκον vocari debere ostenderent. Sed quoniam hujusmodi opinio omnibus odiosa est, nec aliter potest intelligi Θεοτόκος esse Virgo sancta, nisi quis prius crediderit, quod factum sit caro, id est, factum sit homo, Dei Patris Verbum (neque enim divinitatem nudam virgo peperit), quod nobis ex hac contentione emolumenti parient hi, qui certant etiam ἀνθρωποτόκον eam vocari debere?

Verum, quantum apparet, locum sibi adversus Christum dicendi excogitaverunt; non enim patiuntur, vel sentire vel dicere, ipsum Dei Patris Verbum, quod erat ante saecula Filius, novissimis temporibus inconfuse, inconvertibiliterque adunatum esse, ex vulva, carni habenti animam rationabilem, ac sic fuisse hominem similem nostri. Sed sicut unum sanctorum inhabitantem Deum habuisse commemorant, alios etiam ita sentire sollicitant: non considerantes, quod in nobis quoque per sanctum Spiritum, ut in sanctis templis, habitet omnium Deus. Scriptum est enim: Nescitis, quod templum Dei estis, et spiritus Dei habitet in vobis? Si quis ergo templum Dei corrumpit, corrumpet eum Deus; templum enim Dei sanctum est, quod estis vos (I Cor. III, 16). Sed etsi nominati sumus templa, Deum habentes inhabitantem per Spiritum; attamen alium mysterii, secundum Christum, novimus modum: vere enim adunatam esse Deo Verbo dicimus carnem, habentem scilicet animam rationabilem.

Sed libenter eum consulerem, utrum unitatem Dei Verbi et humanitatis, sive sancti corporis rationabiliter animati, factam esse vere confiteatur; an ipse quoque nonnullorum exemplo, per conjunctionem solam, servilis et ἀνυποστάτου formae cum ἐνυποστάτῳ forma divina, sive alio modo, per solam filietatis ὁμωνυμίαν, et aequalitatem dignitatis; aut si alius ullus conjunctionis intelligitur modus? Sed forte sine causa molestus sum, et percunctor non necessario: habeo enim voces ipsius, et apertissimam confessionem; in primo namque hoc capitulo dixit: Ideo natus puer vocatur Emmanuel, nec Deus a natura separatur humana, nec homo divinitate nudus. Oportuerat quidem ipsum subtilem ex his expositionem, elimatamque curare; caeterum id certe notandum est. Ecce enim ipse unitatem explanans, ab humana natura Deum unitate se separare negat, eumdemque confitetur Deum simul et hominem: cur ergo non erubescit, dicta increpans nostra?

ANATHEMATISMUS SECUNDUS.

Siquis non confiteatur, carni per substantiam adunatum esse Dei Patris Verbum, et unum esse Christum cum propria carne, eumdem scilicet Deum simul et hominem; anathema sit.

REPREHENSIO HAERETICI.

Unum quidem Christum confitemur, divinis apostolorum traditionibus obtemperantes, et eumdem propter ἕνωσιν Deum et hominem nominamus. Verum ἕνωσιν per substantiam penitus ignoramus, ut novam, et alienam a divinis Scripturis et Patribus, qui eas interpretati sunt.

Et hic quoque totus locus relatus est damnatusque in V synodo, propterea quod rejiceret ἕνωσιν καθ' ὑπόστασιν, cujus confessio est sola, indubitata, et fraudis expers bene sentiendi regula. Unde canone 13 anathema dicitur ei, qui defenderit impia Theodoreti conscripta, quae contra rectam fidem et contra primam Ephesinam sanctam synodum, et sanctum Cyrillum; et duodecim ejus capitula, exposuit, et omnia quae conscripsit pro Theodoro et Nestorio impiis, et pro aliis, qui eadem praedictis Theodoro et Nestorio sapuerunt, defendens eos, et eorum impietatem, et propter hoc impios vocans doctores Ecclesiae, qui UNITATEM SECUNDUM SUBSISTENTIAM Dei Verbi ad carnem confitentur, etc.

Si autem is, qui haec reperit, vult dicere ἕνωσιν per substantiam, qua commixtio sit facta divinitatis et carnis, contradicemus omni alacritate, et blasphemiam convincemus. Necesse est enim commixtionem confusio sequatur; secuta autem confusio adimit naturae proprietatem: quae enim miscentur, id quod erant ante, non servant; id autem de Deo Verbo et de semine David dicere, flagitiosissimum est. Oportet autem obtemperare Domino demonstranti duas naturas, et dicenti Judaeis: Solvite templum istud, et in triduo reaedificabo ipsum (Joan. II, 19). At si commixtio fuisset facta, nec Deus remansisset Deus, nec templum cognosceretur templum, sed et Deus templum esset, et templum Deus: id enim commixtionis ratio postulat; et non recte Dominus Judaeis dixerit: Solvite templum istud, et in triduo reaedificabo ipsum. Oportuerat enim ita dicere: Solvite me, et in triduo resurgam; siquidem vere commixtio, confusioque fuisset facta: nunc autem ostendit, et templum solvendum, et resuscitaturum Deum. Superflua igitur per substantiam ἕνωσις, qua pro commixtione, ut opinor, utuntur; sufficit autem ἕνωσιν dicere, quae et naturarum proprietates ostendit, et unum adorandum praecipit Christum.

RESPONSIO ORTHODOXI.

Ecce iterum generosus iste barbarus ex minimis causis occasionem maledicendi captans, reprehendit dictionem quod per substantiam dixerimus, et eamdem insolitam esse definit, et novo more eam factam esse a nobis affirmat; nec considerat, quod dictionum vis, impiorum haereticorum argutiis veritatem opponens, convellit id, quod videtur obsistere.

Nestorio igitur ubique evacuante Dei Verbi secundum carnem generationem, et solam dignitatum unitatem nobis instituente, et dicente hominem Deo conjunctum filietatis ὁμωνυμίᾳ fuisse honoratum; necesse fuit, ut nos adversus illius dicta agentes, per substantiam ἕνωσιν factam fuisse diceremus. Hic autem sermo nihil aliud significat, nisi id tantum, quod Verbi natura, sive substantia, id est, ipsum Verbum, humanae naturae vere adunatum, absque omni conversione et confusione, ut saepe diximus, unus intelligatur, et sit Christus, ipse Deus et homo.

Notanda sunt accurate ista Cyrilli verba: τὴν καθ' ὑπόστασιν ἕνωσιν γενέσθαι φαμέν, τοῦ "καθ' ὑπόστασιν" οὐδὲν ἕτερον ἀποφαίνοντος, πλὴν ὅτι μόνον ἡ τοῦ λόγου φύσις, ἤγουν ἡ ὑπόστασις, ὅ ἐστιν αὐτὸς ὁ λόγος, ἀνθρωπείᾳ φύσει κατὰ ἀλήθειαν ἑνωθεὶς, etc. Factam dicimus unitionem secundum ὑπόστασιν; hic autem sermo nihil aliud significat, nisi id tantum, quod Verbi natura, sive hypostasis, id est, ipsum Verbum humanae naturae vere unitum, etc. Inde enim intelligitur famosa illa Athanasii ac Cyrilli sententia: POST UNITIONEM UNA EST VERBI DEI NATURA INCARNATA. Natura enim pro hypostasi posita est; neque illud catholicorum singulare est. Ipse etiam Nestorius, si credimus Patribus V synodi, naturas posuit, pro hypostasibus, cum dixit: Propter eum qui induit, eum qui indutus est, adoro: propter eum qui occultus est, eum qui apparet, adoro. Inseparabilis ab eo, qui apparet, Deus est: propterea ejus, qui inseparabilis est, honorem non separo, separo naturas, sed unio in adoratione (Serm. 7, num. 37). Alteram vero vocem cum altera confudit Theodoretus in reprehensione consequentis anathematismi, cum ait: τῆς τοῦ θείου μορφῆς λαβούσης τὴν τοῦ δούλου μορφήν, ἕν μὲν πρόσωπον, καὶ ἕνα υἱὸν καὶ Χριστὸν ὁμολογεῖν εὐσεβές· δύο δὲ τὰς ἑνωθείσας ὑποστάσεις, εἴτουν φύσεις, λέγειν οὐκ ἄτοπον.

Id autem, ut opinor, Theodoreto ipsi videtur dicenti, ab humana natura Deum non fuisse separatum, nec absque deitate humanitatem intelligi. Igitur nec absque substantiis servi et Dei formas conjunctas dicimus, nec communem hominem aequalitate sola dignitatis honoratum σχετικῶς conjunctum esse Verbo definimus; sed ipsum, ut supra dixi, Filium Dei unigenitum, qui vere carnem assumpsit, quae haberet animam rationabilem, hominem factum, ita tamen ut remaneret et Deus.

Sed vir ille vehemens oratione, et cogitatione acerrimus, commixtionem significari hujusmodi dictione definit, et dicere audet, atque ea, quae ex naturarum commixtione contingant, proponit in medium, quasi nos ignoremus, an forte quadam insolentia gloriatur, et existimat neminem praeter se alium, orationem posse, quantum voluerit, propagare; si modo, quod a nullo sit dictum, tamquam vere dictum, sibi proposuerit, ut aliquid videatur esse apud eos, qui discernere nesciunt, qui sint vaniloqui, mendacesque, et qui rectam viam teneant veritatis, et prudentes exerceant necessariosque sermones.

Opinabar quidem, confiteor, a principio, capitulorum vim ipsum minime ignorasse, sed simulare ignorantiam, et in hoc quibusdam gratificari; vere tamen eum ignorasse nunc comperi.

ANATHEMATISMUS TERTIUS.

Siquis in uno Christo dividat substantias post unitatem, et conjunctione sola conjungat secundum dignitatem, vel auctoritatem, vel dominationem, ac non magis conventione quadam, quae sit facta, per ἕνωσιν naturalem; anathema sit.

REPREHENSIO HAERETICI.

Obscura quidem dictorum caliginosaque sententia; plana vero apud pios ipsorum dementia. Cui enim non sit perspicuum, quod conjunctio et conventio nihil differant? nam et conventio eorum est, quae erant ante divisa. Sed hujusmodi verborum prudentissimus generator, tamquam contraria posuit verba sibi convenientia: Non enim oportet, inquit, conjungere conjunctione substantias; sed complexione, et conventione naturali, aut ignorans forte quid dicat, aut sciendo blasphemans.

Natura enim res est quaedam imperiosa, et cogens quaedam agere, non voluntate. Est autem tale quod dico: Natura esurimus, non voluntate hoc patientes, sed necessitate; ac ni ita esset, pauperes a mendicitate liberarentur, habentes in voluntate sua, ut non esuriant; naturaliter sentimus, naturaliter dormimus, naturaliter spiritum ducimus. Verum haec omnia, sicut dixi, non fiunt voluntate: nam si quis horum aliquid non admittat, necessario vitae sentiet finem. Ergo si naturalis conjunctio facta est formae servilis, compellente quadam necessitate, non sua clementia Deus Verbum conjunctum est formae servili, atque ita invenietur legislator necessariis legibus serviens. Verum non ita nos beatus Paulus edocuit, sed contra magis, quod nempe se exinanivit formam servi accipiens (Philip. II, 6); dicendo, se exinanivit, significat voluntatem. Si igitur suo arbitrio et voluntate, naturae ex nobis assumptae conjunctus est, superflua est dictio naturalis conjunctionis: confiteri enim sufficit ἕνωσιν. ἕνωσις porro de divisis accipitur, nam si nulla sit divisio, numquam ἕνωσις fiet, et qui admittit ἕνωσιν, admittit et divisionem praeviam .

Quare ergo dicit substantias sive naturas dividi non oportere, maxime cum sciat, quod perfecta erat Dei Verbi substantia, quodque perfecta ab eo assumpta forma servilis, ideoque substantias dixerit, et non substantiam? Ergo si utraque natura perfecta est, et ambae in unum convenerunt, Dei forma scilicet formam assumente servilem, unam quidem personam, ἓν μὲν πρόσοπον, et unum Filium ac Christum similiter confiteri, pietatis ratio poscit; duas vero substantias adunatas sive naturas dicere, non ineptum est, sed magis consequens.

Nam si in uno homine naturas dividimus, et mortalem quidem, corpus vocamus; immortalem vero, animam; utrumque autem, hominem: multo magis assumentis Dei, et assumpti hominis naturarum proprietates convenit discernere. Invenimus etiam beatum Paulum, unum eumdemque hominem in duos homines dividentem, et modo dicentem: Quanto exterior homo corrumpitur, tanto interior renovatur (II Cor. IV, 16); modo: Condelector enim legi Dei secundum interiorem hominem (Rom. VII, 22); et statim: In interiore homine inhabitare Christum (Ephes. III, 17). Si igitur naturalem conjunctionem ejusdem temporis naturarum Apostolus dividit, quare impietatis arguit eos qui, dividunt propria naturarum, Dei sempiterni et ejus hominis, qui in novissimis temporibus assumptus est? Arguit, inquam, ille, qui commixtionem nos aliis nominibus docet.

RESPONSIO ORTHODOXI.

Animadverte quomodo sapiens ille vir, primum quidem obscura dicta esse nostra mentitur, et cum ipse caliginosam offusamque habeat mentem, obscurum esse ait tam planum sapientibus, evidentissimumque sermonem.

Arbitratus est autem, quod conventionem, ac non magis conjunctionem, nominari debere, nostra affirmet oratio. Deinde calliditatem suam cupiens ostentare, unum ait a nobis idemque significari, sive conventionem, sive conjunctionem factam esse dicamus. Ego vero hoc quoque loco mentis ipsius acumen admiror: solus enim fortasse didicit quod a nullo est umquam ignoratum; quodque adeo proculcatum est, ut eis etiam, qui sunt omnino a doctrina et litteris saecularibus alienissimi, notissimum videatur; immo et iis qui auditu tantummodo fabularum, ad levem incertamque scientiam pervenerunt.

Admirans igitur ipsius doctrinam, hoc ad eum dico: Vel minimum evigila, velut ex ebrietate aut somno, qui tam magnum in nos os aperire contendis; et animadverte subtiliter acuteque mysterium unitatis, quod de Christo dicitur. Faciunt quidam calumniam huic unitati, in id, quod ipsis libuerit, sacrarum litterarum sententias transferentes: aiunt enim, divisas quidem esse a sese naturas et a sese sejunctas, et seorsus, et in parte sua esse utramque; hominem vero σχετικῶς conjunctum esse Deo contendunt, secundum solam dignitatem, sive auctoritatem et secundum filietatis ὁμωνυμίαν. Huic anathematismus opinioni pugnat, et tam profanis vocum novitatibus reluctatur. Affirmat etenim adunatum fuisse Verbum natura, id est, non σχετικῶς, sed veritate, carni habenti animam rationabilem; et nullo modo dividi oportere, ne duos filios intelligamus, individuum dividentes. At ille non intelligens, quid sit tandem adunatio naturalis, id est, vera, quae neque naturas confundat, nec commixtionem faciat; ita ut utraque aliud esse, quam quod erat, incipiat, infantile aliquid frivolumque assumit ad probationem eorum quae se bene habere arbitratus est.

Denique ait: Si naturalis facta est adunatio; ergo non voluntaria est exinanitus Verbi, sed tamquam ex necessitate, et violentia, imperiosa enim res natura. Ad hoc quilibet ad eum dixerit: Esuritio, et sitis, et caetera, quemadmodum dixisti, carnis sunt infirmitates naturales, et in nobismet ipsis habent motum; propterea quod scilicet naturam passionibus habemus obnoxiam. Divina vero arcanaque Verbi natura non necessitatis, nec passionis capax, omnino a nullo coacta est, ne a se quidem ut contra voluntatem fieret caro, sive assumeret humanitatis mensuram, et Abrahae apprehenderet semen.

Quod vero inconsulta vehementer sit ipsius oratio, non est difficile volentibus invenire: ait enim omnino, et procul dubio, omnia naturalia necessitatis legibus subjacere; et ad hujus rei probationem protulit, nos contra voluntatem esurire atque sitire, ad hoc nos provocante natura, etiamsi quis noluerit (sed erat hominis docti, et in his rebus exercitati solidiores alias rerum causas videre, quae oratione majore requiri dignae sint); nisi forte sit falsum, hominem rationabilem esse natura. Ergo contra voluntatem coactus est rationabilis esse. Deinde, dic mihi, Deus omnipotens nonne natura est Deus? Nonne natura sanctus, justus, bonus, vita, lumen, sapientia, et virtus? Utrum ipse quoque contra voluntatem, et coactus, id est, quod est? Sed ita opinari vesanae stoliditatis est certissimum argumentum.

Quid igitur nobis obtendit mendacium tamquam inexpugnabile, et invincibile munimentum; et tam imbecillis utitur argumentis, ut audiens, naturalem factam esse adunationem, id est, veram, et conversionis liberam, atque inconfusam omnino substantiarum conventionem, torquere conetur vim sententiarum, ut parum recte positae esse credantur? Nec horrescit vir strenuus, naturam Verbi inevitabili necessitati subjacere commemorans. Exinanivit se, non contra voluntatem, sed voluntarius unigenitus factus homo: at non, ut tu ais, assumpsit hominem, σχετικὴν ei praebens conjunctionem, et eum filietatis beneficio honorans, juxta nos.

Ergo, etsi intelligamus adunatas esse substantias, et hominem factum atque incarnatum Dei Verbum: proptereaque videamur, aliquo modo dicere adunationem naturalem, quae illam excludat, quae non est vera, sed σχετικὴ, quamque nos etiam habuimus per fidem et sanctificationem, propterea quod divinae naturae participes fuimus; etenim sicut ait Paulus: Qui adhaeret Domino, unus est Spiritus (I Cor. VI, 17); non tamen necessitati et violentiae naturali impassibile et liberum Dei Verbum subjicimus.

Quod vero post adunationem nolumus ea, quae adunata sunt, a sese esse sejuncta, nisi fallor, nec criminosum omnino est, nec culpabile videtur, cum praesertim ipse vir egregius Theodoretus unum ex nobis hominem exempli causa proponens, in duo dividi non sinat; quamvis quantum ad hominis θεωρίαν pertinet, divisionis patiens esse possit, eo videlicet, quod intelligimus, aliud animam esse natura, aliud natura propria carnem. Ergo simili ratione curiosius inquirentes, adunationem, quae in Christo facta esse intelligitur, secundum θεωρίαν quidem divinitatis et humanitatis, conventionem veram per ἕνωσιν factam esse dicimus: non ignorantes, aliud quidem esse praeter carnem Dei Verbum, aliam vero juxta suam naturam carnem, praeter Verbum. Adunatum vero semel dividere criminosum est; nec in duos Filios separare unum Christum, et Filium, et Dominum recta ratio permittit: in hanc enim scientiam nos sancta et divina Scriptura deducit.

Verum ille dogmatum veritatis nullam habet penitus curam, nec laborat discere aliquid necessarium, et quod vel mediocriter ipsi prodesse possit, sed id tantum, quod nocere possit. Verumtamen cum mendacio glorietur, et calumniandi jactet se habere calliditatem, audiat a nobis: Quid gloriaris in malitia, qui potens es in iniquitate? tota die injustitiam cogitavit lingua tua (Psal. LI, 3).

ANATHEMATISMUS QUARTUS.

Siquis personis duabus, sive substantiis dispertiat voces, quae sunt in evangelicis, vel apostolicis Scripturis, quaeque vel de Christo a sanctis dicuntur, vel ab ipso de se ipso, et has quidem, ut homini, qui praeter Verbum seorsus intelligatur, deputet; has vero, ut divinas, soli Deo Verbo; anathema sit.

REPREHENSIO HAERETICI.

Cognata haec quoque supradictis: vult enim, tamquam commixtione facta, nullam esse verborum differentiam, quae in sacris Evangeliis, sive apostolicis libris, dicta sunt; cum praesertim Ario, et Eunomio, et caeteris haerese ὠν auctoribus hostem se esse glorietur.

Dicat igitur divinorum dogmatum peritissimus magister, quomodo haereticorum blasphemiam possit arguere, humilia et servi formae verba convenientia Deo deputans Verbo: illi enim hoc facientes, et minorem, et creaturam, et facturam, et servum, et ex nihilo factum, Filium asserunt Dei.

Cui igitur nos, qui ab illis diversa sentimus, et qui ejusdem substantiae coaeternum cum Deo et Patre Filium confitemur, opificem omnium, et factorem, et ordinatorem, et gubernatorem, et arbitrum sapientissimum, et omnipotentem, immo vero ipsam per se virtutem, ipsam vitam, ipsam sapientiam. Cui, inquam, haec deputemus: Deus, Deus meus, ob quid me dereliquisti (Matth. XXVII, 46); et illud: Pater, si potest fieri, transeat a me calix iste (Matth. XXVI, 39); et: Pater, salva me ab hora ista (Joan. XII, 27); et illud: Horam illam nemo scit, nec Filius hominis (Marc. XIII, 32), et caetera, quae humiliter ab ipso dicta sunt, et a sanctis apostolis de ipso conscripta sunt? Cui esuritionem ascribamus? Cui fatigationem et somnum? Cui ignorantiam et timiditatem? Quis est, qui adjutorio eguit angelorum? Si haec Dei Verbi sunt, quomodo sapientia ignoravit? Vel quomodo sapientia nominatur, quae ignorantiae habeat vitium? Vel quomodo verum dixisse videbitur, omnia Patris se habere commemorans, cum non habeat Patris scientiam? Solus enim, inquit, Pater scit diem illam (Matth. XXIV, 36). Vel quomodo imago sit simillima genitoris, qui non omnia habeat genitoris? Si non mentitur dicens se ignorare, haec quis de ipso existimaverit; sin vero novit diem, et occultare volens ignorare se dicit: vides qualis ex hoc blasphemia consequatur; veritas scilicet mentitur. Sed qui veritas vocetur, quae contrarium habeat veritati? Si non mentitur veritas, neque Deus Verbum ignorat diem, quam ipse disposuit, in qua judicaturus est orbem terrarum, sed habet Patris scientiam, quippe imago simillima. Ergo non Dei Verbi est ignorantia, sed servilis formae, quae illo tempore tanta sciebat, quanta inhabitans deitas revelabat.

Et id quoque fere totum, quod paragrapho continetur, relatum est in V synodo, velut Nestoriano errore, de duobus filiis, infectum, quod advertit Cyrillus.

Hoc de aliis similibus potest dici: quid enim habet rationis, Dei Verbum dicere ad Patrem: Pater, si potest fieri, transeat a me calix iste; verumtamen non sicut ego volo, sed sicut tu (Matth. XXVI, 39)? Ex hoc enim rursus irrationabilia multa eveniunt; et primum, discordare Patrem et Filium, et alia velle Patrem, alia Filium, ait enim: Verumtamen non sicut ego volo, sed sicut tu. Deinde ingentem rursus ignorantiam in Filio esse videbimus, invenietur enim ignorans dicere: Si potest fieri, transeat calix. Hoc autem de Deo Verbo dicere impium est, et blasphemiae plenum: sciebat enim certissime, qui hujus causa advenit, qui sponte nostram naturam assumpsit, qui se exinanivit, dispensationis mysterii exitum, propter quem sanctis praedicabat apostolis: Ecce ascendimus Hierosolymam, et Filius hominis tradetur in manus gentium, et flagellabitur, et crucifigetur, et tertia die resurget (Matth. XX, 1). Qui igitur haec pronuntiavit, et qui Petrum objurgavit deprecantem ne fieret, quomodo deprecatus esset ne fieret, si plane sciebat omne futurum? Quomodo autem non sit absurdum, Abraham quidem ante multa saecula vidisse diem ipsius, et gratulatum esse; et Isaiam item praecantasse salutares passiones, et Jeremiam, et Danielem, et Zachariam, et omnem prophetarum chorum; ipsum vero et ignorare, et liberationem poscere, et deprecari id, quod saluti mundi fuerat profuturum? Ergo non Dei Verbi ista sunt verba, sed servi formae, quae pavebat mortem, quia nondum mors fuerat resoluta; sed Deus Verbum haec dicere concessit, dans locum timiditati, ut appareret geniti natura, et ne δόκημα et φαντασίαν, id quod ex Abraham et David factum est, existimemus, ob profanos haereticos, quorum factio talem blasphemiam peperit.

Ergo ea, quae divine dicta, vel facta sunt, Deo Verbo ascribamus; quae vero humiliter dicta sunt, servi formae aptemus, ne Arii et Eunomii blasphemias aemulemur.

RESPONSIO ORTHODOXI.

Nonne multo melius, quaeso, fuerat ipsum, vim perscrutari dictorum, ab odio et praejudicio liberum animum retinentem? Verum id minime agere dignatur; omnia enim ad suum convertit arbitrium, et ait: Cognata et haec supradictis: vult enim, tamquam commixtione facta, nullam esse verborum differentiam, quae in sanctis evangeliis vel apostolicis dictis conscripta sunt; cum praesertim Ario, et Eunomio, et caeteris haerese ω n auctoribus hostem se esse glorietur. Et haec quidem ille: verum tantum abest, ut ego dicam naturas inter se fuisse confusas, et confusionem, commixtionem ac conversionem suscepisse, quantum abest, ut ille recta sentiat.

Sed neque verborum quidem differentiam sustulimus: scimus enim, haec quidem divine facta esse, haec vero humane; et quod haec excellentissimae conveniant gloriae, haec sint exinanitatis aptiora mensurae. Oportere autem asserimus, ea personis duabus a se penitus divisis non deputari: nam si est unus Dominus noster Jesus Christus, una fides in ipsum, et unum baptisma (Ephes. IV, 5), una erit et unius ipsius recte persona. Et si erit ipse Deus simul et homo, decet ipsum certe et divine simul facere et humane sermones; cum neque inde divina ipsius arcanaque natura ulla ex particula fiat majestate Patris inferior; et illa dispensatio cum carne credenda sit, quod cum sit Deus, homo etiam juxta nos factus dicatur.

Omnia igitur unius Christi sunt, divina atque humana: nam si non factum est homo Dei Patris Verbum, non juxta nos sane loquatur humane; sin autem verum est, ipsum similiter ac nos communicasse sanguini et carni, assimilans se per omnia fratribus, nobis scilicet; quare dispensationis rectissimam rationem stultissime reprehendunt, qui vocem non patiuntur humanam, quique sermonis, propter dispensationem factam, humilitatem, tamquam alii seorsum Filio, servi formae, ut ipsi aiunt, deputare festinant?

Ineptum est autem, eos haereticorum quidem malignitatem horrere se dicere; rectae autem fidei traditionem nolle sectari: praestabilius autem sit, et multo doctius, voces humanas aptare, non alii personae, quae intelligatur seorsus Filius, et servi formae, sicut ipsi dicere consueverunt; sed magis humanitatis ipsius deputare mensurae: decuerat enim, cum esset Deus simul et homo, per utrosque eum procedere sermones.

Admiror autem, quod simulet quidem ipse quoque, confiteri, quod sit unus Christus, idem scilicet Deus simul et homo; deinde tamquam in oblivionem delapsus eorum, quae recte habere arbitratus est, unum dividat rursus in duo. Ponit enim Salvatoris vocem dicentis: De die autem aut hora illa nemo scit, nec angeli coelorum, nec Filius, nisi Pater (Marc. XIII, 32). Deinde sapientiam esse affirmans Dei Patris Verbum, et omnia futura praescire, adjicit et ait: Non ergo Dei Verbi ignorantia, sed servi formae, quae tanta eo tempore sciebat; haec et de aliis similibus dici possunt. Ergo si non mendaciter dicis unum Christum, et Deum Filium, eumdem Deum simul et hominem: quare dividis, et duos dicere Filios non erubescis, nisi forte non videantur duo esse omnino, is qui habeat scientiam praefinitam, et is qui omnia sciat, et qui particularem accipiat revelationem, et qui sit perfectus sapientia, et tanta cognoscat, quanta etiam Pater?

Si autem est unus et idem, propter adunationis verissimae rationem, et non alius et alius divise et separatim, ipsius est omnino scire et videri nescire. Ergo scit quidem divine, utpote sapientia Patris. Sed quoniam inscitae humanitatis mensuram subit dispensatorie, et hoc quoque cum aliis familiare facit; quamvis sicut nuper diximus, nihil prorsus ignoret, sed sciat cuncta cum Patre.

Quam igitur ob causam esurisse dicitur, et fatigatus esse ex itinere, cum sit vita et vivificus, utpote Deus, et cum sit ipse panis vivus, qui de coelo descendit, et vitam dans mundo (Joan. VI, 51), et ipse sit idem virtutum Dominus (Psal. XXIII, 10)? Scilicet ut factus fuisse homo vere credatur, familiaria putat humana, numquam naturae suae bonis excedens; sed ea immota retinens, in quibus erat semper, et est, et erit.

Qui vero revelationem datam esse commemorat servi formae a Deo inhabitante, et eam praefinitam, Prophetam nobis ostendit Emmanuel, et hominem Θεοφόρον, et aliud nihil.

Verum callidum aliquid se dicere et inexpugnabile arbitratur: Nam si Dei Verbum, inquit, est quod exclamavit, PATER, SI POTEST FIERI, TRANSEAT A ME CALIX ISTE (Matth. XXVI, 39).

Primum quidem a Patre discordat, nec recte recusat bibere calicem; cum sciat, inquit, quod mundo salutaris futura fuerat passio: igitur non sunt, inquit, Dei Verbi tales voces. Audiat igitur contra super hoc quoque a nobis, qui tam infirmis rationibus nutat et titubat. Ergo quoniam tibi videntur tales voces a Deo Verbo removeri debere, et soli deputari formae servili, nonne in duos filios unum dividis, et cui hoc sapientium videtur obscurum? Dixerit enim fortasse aliquis, tuas sequens rationes, quod nec verisimile sit, nec rationabile, recusare passionem servi formam, et discordare a Patre, et ab eo, quod inhabitaverat, Verbo, cum sciret passionem salutarem mundo futuram, et vitae causam illis, qui fuerant morte devicti. Oportebat ergo, inquit, ipsam videri timiditate superiorem, et divinis imperiis obtemperantem Nonne igitur te sentis frustra garrire? Unde haec sententiarum vulgaris inventio

Ergo, quod omnia quidem humana Deo Verbo parvula et exigua videantur, sane confiteor; sed requiro, exinanitas cujus facta esse intelligatur, et quis volens eam sustinuerit. Nam si, ut ipsi aiunt, servi forma, sive id quod erat ex semine David; quomodo et qua ratione exinanitum sit, cum a Deo assumptum sit? Si vero ipsum Verbum, quod erat in forma et aequalitate Dei et Patris, exinanisse se dicitur, quomodo rursus vel qua ratione exinanitum sit, si recuset exinanitatem? Exinanitas autem Dei Verbi, quod nescit pati conversionem, est agere aliquid vel dicere humanorum, propter conventionem dispensatoriam carnis.

Sed etsi factus sit homo, nullo tamen modo naturam ejus mysterii violat ratio: mansit enim id quod erat, etiamsi ad humanitatem, propter mundi salutem, vitamque descenderit. Igitur non personis duabus, sed uni Christo, Filioque et Deo, evangelicas ac sanctorum apostolorum deputabimus voces; neque divinam ipsius naturam, et gloriam minorem facientes, propter humanam, nec dispensationem abnuentes; sed ipsius Verbi ἐνανθρώπησιν propter nos factam esse credentes.

ANATHEMATISMUS QUINTUS.

Siquis dicere audeat, Christum esse hominem θεοφόρον, ac non magis vere Deum, utpote unum filium per naturam, eo quod Verbum factum sit caro, et communicarit similiter ac nos carni et sanguini; anathema sit.

REPREHENSIO HAERETICI.

Communicasse quidem similiter ac nos, sanguini et carni, et animae immortali Deum Verbum, eo quod haec ipsi sint adunata, confitemur. Carnem vero Deum Verbum conversione factum esse, non dicimus; sed illos etiam, qui id dicunt, impietatis arguimus. Quam autem contrarium id sit jam ante dictis, videre licet: nam si Verbum in carnem conversum est, non communicavit certe carni et sanguini; sin autem carni et sanguini communicavit, quasi alius praeter haec, communicavit: si vero caro aliud est praeter ipsum, non est ipsum in carnem conversum. Ergo nomine communicationis utentes, ut unum quidem Filium adoramus, et eum, qui assumpsit, et eum, qui assumptus est; differentiam tamen cognoscimus naturarum.

Θεοφόρον autem, id est, deiferum, dicere, ut a multis sanctis Patribus dictus est, non recusamus: quorum unus magnus ille Basilius, in oratione ad Amphilochium de sancto Spiritu, hoc est usus nomine, et in interpretatione psalmi quinquagesimi noni. Vocamus autem θεοφόρον, non ut particularem nescio quam divinam gratiam accipientem, sed ut omnem habentem adunatam Filii deitatem; hoc enim explanans beatus Paulus dicebat: Videte, ne quis nos seducat, propter philosophiam et inanem gloriam, secundum traditionem hominum, secundum elementa mundi, et non secundum Christum; quia in ipso inhabitat omnis plenitudo divinitatis corporaliter (Coloss. II, 8).

RESPONSIO ORTHODOXI.

Hic quoque vanas eum fabulas exercere nullus est labor ostendere; asserimus enim, a nullo oportere θεοφόρον hominem nominari Christum, ne juxta unum aliquem intelligatur fuisse sanctorum; sed Deum magis verum hominem factum, et incarnatum Dei Verbum.

Increpat autem iterum, quae recte sunt dicta, et fallit modis variis, atque mentitur. Ait, dicere nos, in naturam carnis Dei Verbum fuisse conversum, et eruit rationes ex alto, per quas probare contendit Dei Verbum non esse vertibile. Quod vero saepius dixi, dicam nunc quoque necessario, cum nemo sit, qui in carnem terrenam, divinam immortalemque Verbi naturam conversam fuisse dicat; sed inconvertibilem eam omnes confiteantur. Parcite jam inanes labores impendere, ut eis, qui in nullo decepti sunt, possitis ostendere, quod et invertibile sit per naturam, et incommutabile Dei Verbum. Quis enim adeo stupidus, vel mente captus est, qui tam dedecorosa, et ipsis forte etiam insipientibus abominanda, sentire velit et dicere?

Ego vero vehementer admiror, quod cum ubique affirmet, Deum esse Emmanuel, Prophetae ei mensuram in his tribuisse convincatur: ait enim, ipsum esse hominem θεοφόρον, ut videatur esse juxta nos, qui habemus inhabitantem Deum in nobis per sanctum Spiritum: inhabitat enim in cordibus nostris, et sumus templa Dei. Minime vero tantumdem est, dicere Verbum factum esse hominem, ac Deum in homine inhabitare; nam licet vera sit beati Pauli vox: Quoniam in ipso complacuit inhabitare omnem plenitudinem divinitatis corporaliter (Coloss. II, 8), id est, non σχετικῶς; attamen unum ait esse Patrem, et unum Dominum Jesum Christum, per quem omnia.

Dicat aliquis deinde, etiam in homine inhabitare Christum, ejusdemque spiritum, et scriptum esse de quibusdam: Inhabitantes autem domos luteas (Job. IV, 19); de quibus et nos ex eodem luto sumus: attamen unus intelligitur, et est per compositionem homo ex carne, et ex anima rationabili carnem inhabitante. Cur ergo rectam et stabilem fidei rationem turbare non cessat? Modo enim unum ait Christum, et Filium, et Dominum, eumdemque Deum simul et hominem: modo inter prophetas eum ponit, hominem ipsum nominans θεοφόρον, nesciens se fortasse ipsum aequare, vel ipsis nobis, si quidem non sit Deus vere, sed magis templum, in quo inhabitet Verbum, sicut et in nobis. Verum haec non ita se habere, divina Scriptura perdocuit: Verbum caro factum est, et habitavit in nobis (Joan. I, 14); ne quis arbitretur per conversionem et commutationem in carnis naturam ipsum fuisse conversum. Qui autem factus est caro, sive homo, non est homo θεοφόρος, sed Deus magis, qui se in voluntariam exinanitatem immisit, et propriam carnem fecit ex muliere, carnem autem non inanimem et absque sensu, sed animatam et rationabilem.

Meminimus autem, et templum eum nominasse suum corpus: caeterum non σχετικὴν fecit inhabitationem, sicut et in nobis, per spiritum; sed unus per adunationem intelligitur Christus, et Filius, et Dominus.

ANATHEMATISMUS SEXTUS.

Siquis dicat, Deum vel Dominum esse Christi, Dei Patris Verbum; ac non magis confitetur eumdem Deum simul et hominem, propterea quod Verbum caro sit factum, secundum Scripturas; anathema sit.

REPREHENSIO HAERETICI.

Beatus quidem Paulus id, quod a Deo Verbo assumptum est, formam nominat servi. Sed quoniam ante adunationem assumptio est; de assumptione autem beatus Paulus disputans, servi formam vocavit assumptam naturam: ideo nullum jam locum habet, adunatione facta, servitutis nomen; nam si eis, qui in ipsum crediderunt, beatus Paulus scribens dicebat: Ergo jam non est servus, sed Filius (Gal. IV, 7); et Dominus porro discipulis: Non jam dicam vos servos, sed amicos (Joan. XV, 15); multo magis primordium nostrae naturae, per quod etiam nos adoptionis meruimus gratiam, servili appellatione liberatum est.

Deum igitur confitemur servi formam, propter adunatam ei formam Dei, et assentimus Prophetae vocanti puerum Emmanuel, et magni consilii nuntium, et miraculum, et consiliarium, et Deum fortem, et dominantem, et principem pacis, et patrem futuri saeculi (Isai. VII, 14; IX, 6). Idem vero propheta etiam post adunationem, praedicans assumpti naturam, servum appellat id quod est ex semine Abraham, ita dicens: Servus meus es tu Israel, et in te gloriabor (Is. XLIX, 3); et rursus: Ita dixit Dominus, qui me finxit ex utero servum sibi (Ibid. 5). Et paulo post: Ecce dedi te in testamentum generis in lumen gentium, ut esses in salutem usque ad extremum terrae (Isai. XLII, 7; XLIX, 6). Quod autem in utero fictum est, non est Deus Verbum, sed servi forma: neque enim Deus Verbum conversum factum est caro, sed assumpsit carnem habentem animam rationabilem.

RESPONSIO ORTHODOXI.

Mysterium dispensationis Unigeniti, quae cum carne facta est, nostros sermones nihilo nunc minus communiet, et eos non irrationabiliter habitos facillime demonstrabit: qui enim in forma est Dei et Patris unigenitus Filius, qui per omnia est aequalis genitori, qui ejusdem gloriae, et liber, servi formam accipiens, nuncupatus est frater eorum, qui jugum ferunt servitutis, id est, noster. Itaque tamquam unus ex nobis didragmum tributorum exactoribus pensitabat, et factus est sub lege ut homo, qui est legislator ut Deus; edocebat autem tunc suos discipulos, quod et Filius sit vere, et in forma servi propter carnem, cumque per suam naturam sit liber, utpote ex Deo, et Deus; verumtamen, propriam habens servi formam, propter exinanitatis mensuram, tributum exactoribus pensitabat.

Ergo etiamsi quispiam dixerit, servum eum fuisse nominatum prophetarum voce sanctorum, nullo modo debet quisquam scandalum pati: sciebant enim illi, revelante Spiritu sancto, quod factum homo, quod ex Deo Patre Verbum, erat quidem, sic quoque liber Filius; non tamen sapientissimae exinanitatis abjiciebat mensuram, nobis qui sumus sub servitutis jugo, similem capiens formam. Sic et Deum ipsum Patrem dicit, cum ipse natura sit Deus et ex Patre; et nulla parte majestate Patris inferior est.

Nestorio igitur scribente ita de Christo: Ergo qui passus est, est ille pontifex misericors, non Deus vivificator ejus, qui passus est, Verbum Christi nominante Deum, atque haec adjiciente: Erat autem ipse et puer, et pueri Dominus (Serm. 6, num. 6); nec recte, nec competenti modo, sed impie dictos esse hos sermones, vehementer affirmamus. Nam si Christi Deus est Verbum Dei et Patris, duo omnino, et procul dubio esse necesse est. Quo autem modo intelligatur idem, et puer, et pueri Dominus? Non ergo dicendus est et Deus sui, et Dominus Emmanuel, siquidem est idem, et Deus simul et homo, quasi homo factum et incarnatum Dei Verbum. Quod vero divinitas quidem aliud quiddam sit natura sua, aliud humanitas, nemo possit ambigere: caeterum ex utraque est Christus, ex deitate et humanitate, secundum dispensatoriam adunationem.

ANATHEMATISMUS SEPTIMUS.

Siquis Christum, ut hominem, operatione Dei Verbi adjutum dicat, et illi gloriam Unigeniti, ut alii praeter ipsum, assignet; anathema sit.

REPREHENSIO HAERETICI.

Si mortalis est hominis natura, Deique Verbum, cum vita sit atque vivificum, suscitavit templum, quod a Judaeis solutum est, et elevavit in coelos, quomodo non glorificata est servi forma per Dei formam? Nam si quae natura mortalis est, facta est immortalis, propter adunationem Verbi et Dei, id quod non habebat accepit; accipiens autem quod non habebat, et glorificata, ab eo qui dedit, glorificata est; propter quod Apostolus clamat: Secundum operationem potestatis virtutis ipsius, quam operatus est in Christo, suscitans eum a mortuis (Eph. I, 20).

RESPONSIO ORTHODOXI.

Qui Christum nominant, non unum similem nostri communem hominem, sed hominem factum, et incarnatum Dei Verbum audientibus designant. Ergo, etsi aliquid mirabilium et divinorum operum dicatur per suum corpus implesse, quod ei instrumenti praebuit officium, nihilominus tamen ipse est, qui operatur, virtutum Dominus Christus, principatum non alii praestans, ut operari possit; sicut nempe beatis discipulis potestatem praebebat spiritus immundos, ut eos ejicerent, et curarent omnem morbum, et omnem infirmitatem in populo. Unde beatus Paulus dicebat: Non enim audeo aliquid loqui eorum, quae per me non effecit Christus, verbo et factis, in virtute signorum et prodigiorum, in virtute Spiritus sancti (Rom. XV, 18). Gaudentes etiam beati discipuli accedebant aliquando ad Christum dicentes: Domine, etiam daemonia nobis subdita sunt in nomine tuo (Luc. X, 17).

Adjutos quidem per Christum in spiritu dicimus sanctos, quasi alios praeter ipsum. An non eodem modo, eademque ratione et ipsum adjutum Jesum a Verbo in spiritu, intelligimus, quasi alium Filium praeter Filium Dei unigenitum? Unum enim ipsum adunatio nobis ostendit, et in duo dividere recusamus: nam etsi caro factum sit Verbum, juxta Scripturas, attamen est sic quoque Filius unigenitus, secundum adunationem veram, quam nemo cogitatione capiat mentis.

Ipse igitur unus est solus Christus Jesus, qui per suum corpus, tamquam per instrumentum, operatus est signa divina. Nec ipsum Christum dicimus operatione adjutum, exemplo sanctorum: hoc enim impium est et vehementer culpabile. Sed si suscitavit a mortuis proprium corpus, utpote vita ipse, et vivificus, illudque glorificavit, vivificam suam naturam esse demonstrans, at non alii cuidam praeter se in hoc gloriam donavit. Certe quidem ad coelestem Patrem dicebat: Pater glorifica me gloria, quam habui penes te, priusquam mundus fieret (Joan. XVII, 5); tametsi et Deus esset, et ex Deo per naturam, gloriaeque Dominus. Quo igitur modo, quasi gloriae egenus, quam habebat ante mundum, gloriam reposcit? Nam postquam factus est homo, etiam per suam carnem: Gratia Dei pro omnibus mortem gustavit (Heb. II, 9), ut ait beatus Paulus. Exinde ortae injuriae recusans opprobrium, praenuntiat resurrectionem, per quam cognoscitur, quod sit et vita, et vivificus, utpote Deus, et eo quoque modo a nobis creditur.

Glorificavit igitur non alium quemdam, sed semetipsum, templum sibi vere conjunctum designans morte validius; corpus autem, quod est ipsi adunatum, non inanimum, nec absque sensu et mente esse credimus.

ANATHEMATISMUS OCTAVUS.

Siquis dicere audeat, assumptum hominem coadorari oportere cum Deo Verbo, et conglorificari, et connuncupari Deum, tamquam alterum cum altero;

ac non magis una veneratione colit Emmanuel, et unam ei glorificationem deputat, eo quod Verbum caro factum est (Joan. I, 14); anathema sit.

REPREHENSIO HAERETICI.

Unam quidem, ut saepe dixi, glorificationem offerimus Domino Christo, et eumdem Deum simul et hominem confitemur: hoc enim nos adunationis ratio docuit, at naturarum proprietates dicere non recusabimus. Neque enim Deus Verbum in carnem conversum est; nec rursus homo, id quod fuerat, perdidit, et in Dei naturam transmutatus est; ergo utriusque naturae proprietatem dicentes, Christum Dominum adoramus.

RESPONSIO ORTHODOXI.

At nos meliora magisque vera sentire soliti, et subtiliores sensus tractantes ad certiorem explanationem, rectioremque mysterii, juxta litterarum praecepta sacrarum, et juxta morem Patrum sanctorum, non hominem assumptum dicimus a Deo Verbum, et ei conjunctum, per σχέσιν extrinsecus intelligendam; sed hominem magis ipsum factum esse definimus. Hujus causa eos, qui dicere audent, assumptum fuisse hominem, ducimus esse extra terminos dogmatum pietatis, qui affirmant ipsum, ut alterum cum altero, coadorari debere cum Filio Dei: nam si est idem Deus, simul et homo, adoratur magis, ut unus, adoratione una, ac non coadoratur, et connuncupatur Deus, ne homo simpliciter communis, et similis nostri Emmanuel esse credatur, per beneficium divinae gloriae particeps factus: creditur enim magis Deus in carne propter nos vere homo factus, non conversione naturae, aut commutatione, sed adunatione dispensatoria.

ANATHEMATISMUS NONUS.

Siquis dicat unum Dominum Jesum Christum, glorificatum ab Spiritu virtute ipsius, quasi aliena vi, et ab ipso accipere, ut possit operari adversus immundos spiritus, et implere signa divina, ac non magis ipsius esse proprium spiritum, per quem operatus est signa divina; anathema sit.

REPREHENSIO HAERETICI.

Hic plane non eos tantum, qui in hoc saeculo pietatem servant, sed illos etiam, qui ante fuerunt, praedicatores veritatis, et ipsos divinorum Evangeliorum scriptores, ac sanctorum apostolorum chorum; praeterea etiam Gabriel archangelum anathematizare ausus est. Secundum carnem enim Christum ex Spiritu sancto factum esse, primus ille, et ante conceptionem praedixit Mariae; et post conceptionem Joseph edocuit, ad Mariam quidem interrogantem: Quomodo erit mihi istud, quoniam virum non cognosco (Luc. I, 35)? dicens: Spiritus sanctus superveniet in te, et virtus Altissimi obumbrabit tibi, propterea quod nascetur sanctum, vocabitur Filius Dei. Ad Joseph vero: Ne timeas accipere Mariam conjugem tuam, quod enim in ea natum est, ex Spiritu sancto est (Matth. I, 20). Et Evangelista: Desponsata autem, inquit, matre ejus Maria Joseph, inventa est in utero habens de Spiritu sancto (Ibid., 18). Et ipse etiam Dominus ingressus in synagogam Judaeorum, cum accepisset Isaiam prophetam, et legisset illum locum, in quo ait: Spiritus Domini super me, cujus causa unxit me (Luc. IV, 18); et quae sequuntur, adjecit: Hodie impleta est scriptura haec in auribus vestris (Ibid., 21). Id autem et beatus Petrus, cum ad Judaeos loqueretur, dixit: Jesum de Nazareth, quem unxit Deus Spiritu sancto (Act. X, 38); et Isaias ante multa saecula praecantavit: Exiit virga de radice Jesse, et flos de radice ejus ascendet, et requiescet supra ipsum spiritus Dei, spiritus sapientiae et intellectus, spiritus consilii et virtutis, spiritus scientiae et pietatis; spiritus timoris Dei replebit eum (Isai. XI, 1). Et rursus: Ecce filius meus quem dilexi; dilectus meus, in quo complacuit anima mea. Ponam spiritum meum super eum, et judicium gentibus annuntiabit (Matth. XII, 18). Id autem testimonium etiam Evangelista in suis scriptis posuit; ipse autem Dominus in evangeliis ad Judaeos dixit: Sin autem in spiritu Dei ego ejicio daemonia, sane pervenit in vos regnum Dei (Luc. XI, 20). Et Joannes: Qui misit me, inquit, baptizare in aqua, ipse mihi dixit: Super quem videris Spiritum descendentem, et manentem super ipsum, ipse est, qui baptizat in Spiritu sancto (Joan. I, 33).

Igitur non prophetas solos, et apostolos, nec solum Gabriel archangelum, anathematizavit ille divinorum dogmatum diligentissimus examinator; verum etiam in ipsum Salvatorem omnium protendit blasphemiam. Ostendimus enim, et ipsum Christum, modo quidem Judaeis, postquam recitasset: Spiritus Domini super me, propter quod unxit me; dixisse: Hodie scriptura haec impleta est in auribus vestris (Luc. IV, 18); modo ad eos, qui dixerant, ipsum per Beelzebuth ejicere daemonia, dixisse, in spiritu Dei se ejicere daemonia (Luc. XI, 20).

Formatum vero a sancto Spiritu, unctumque non dicimus Deum Verbum, quod est cum Spiritu ejusdem substantiae, et coaeternum; sed naturam humanam, quae ab ipso novissimis est assumpta temporibus.

Proprium vero spiritum Filii, si quia ejusdem naturae sit, et ex Patre exeat, dixit, consentiemus, et ut piam vocem accipiemus; sin autem quia ex Filio, vel per Filium, habeat exstantiam, id ut blasphemiam, et impietatem projiciemus. Credimus enim Domino dicenti: Spiritus, qui ex Patre exit (Joan. XV, 26); divino Paulo item dicenti: Nos autem non spiritum mundi accepimus, sed spiritum qui ex Patre est (I Cor. II, 12).

RESPONSIO ORTHODOXI.

Jam ante dixi, quod Nestorii vanitatibus, immo blasphemiis, et dictis ipsius vehementer incultis, capitulorum vis repugnat. Illo enim dicente de Spiritu sancto (Serm. 2): Hic qui tantam Christo gloriam condonavit, qui eum daemoniis fecit horribilem, qui assumptionem ipsi in coelos donavit; et de Christo, tamquam de aliquo homine communi simili nostri, haec ita garriente, factus est necessario anathematismus. Non in eos, qui dicunt, glorificatum esse a sancto Spiritu Jesum, id est, hominem factum Dei Verbum; sed in illos magis, qui impudenter ipsum virtute Spiritus sancti, tamquam aliena, usum fuisse commemorant. Meminimus enim ejus evidenter dicentis de Spiritu sancto: Ille me glorificabit (Joan. XVIII, 14). Novimus praeterea sancti Spiritus operatione immundos malignosque spiritus ipsum contundere.

Sed non dicimus, tamquam unum quempiam prophetarum, usum fuisse ipsum virtute Spiritus sancti, ut aliena: erat namque ipsius, et est, Spiritus sanctus, sicut et Patris. Hoc autem nobis evidentissime designavit divinus Paulus ita scribens: Qui autem in carne sunt, Deo placere non possunt; vos autem non estis in carne, sed in spiritu, si quidem spiritus Dei inhabitat in vobis. Si quis autem Spiritum Christi non habet, hic non est ejus (Rom. IV, 9). Exit namque ex Deo et Patre Spiritus sanctus, secundum Salvatoris vocem, sed non est a Filio alienus: omnia enim habet cum Patre. Et id ipse ostendit de Spiritu sancto: Omnia quae habet Pater, mea sunt, ideo dixi vobis, quod ex meo accipiet, et annuntiabit vobis (Joan. XVI, 15). Glorificavit igitur Jesum Spiritus sanctus mirabilia operantem; verumtamen ut spiritus ipsius, nec aliena virtute, nec ipso melior, eo quod intelligitur Deus.

Non blasphemavimus ergo in angelos sanctos, nec in prophetas, ut ausus est dicere, qui maledicere tantum didicit. Verum, quoniam adhuc propositum est ei, et similibus ipsius, unum Christum in duos dividere; in eum nempe, qui glorificatur, et eum qui operationem adjuvat: reprehendunt insipienter omnem rationem pietatis, quae eos possit a tam prava opinione reducere.

Denique de beato Gabriel mentionem faciens objurgator: Illum qui secundum carnem, inquit, Christum ex Spiritu sancto factum fuisse, primus ille et ante conceptionem praedixit. Alius est igitur Christus, qui secundum carnem; et alius specialiter Christus, qui ex Deo Patre Verbum. Ubi ergo adunatio? Et quod erit inde emolumentum, si duo sunt Christi, et seorsum uterque intelligitur et vocatur?

Licet ergo vultum personamque pietatis sibi fingentes, unum Christum dicant, duos tamen credentes audiant a nobis: Quousque claudicabitis utroque pede (III Reg. XVIII, 21)? Melius est enim rectis uti vestigiis, rectam fidem servantes et stabilem, ac non ineptis cogitationibus vacillantem.

ANATHEMATISMUS DECIMUS.

Pontificem et apostolum confessionis nostrae factum esse Christum, divina Scriptura commemorat. Obtulit enim se ipse pro nobis in odorem suavitatis Deo et Patri. Si quis igitur pontificem, et apostolum nostrum factum esse dicat, non ipsum Verbum Dei, tunc scilicet, cum est caro factum, et homo juxta nos; sed ut alium, praeter ipsum, seorsum hominem ex muliere: aut si quis dicat, pro se obtulisse ipsum oblationem, ac non magis pro nobis tantummodo, neque enim eguit sacrificio, qui peccatum non noverat; anathema sit.

REPREHENSIO HAERETICI.

Non in carnis naturam inconvertibilis natura conversa est; sed humanam naturam assumpsit, eamque super communes pontifices constituit, sicut beatus Paulus docet dicens: Omnis namque pontifex ex hominibus assumptus, pro hominibus constituitur in his, quae sunt ad Deum, ut offerat dona et sacrificia pro peccatis, qui condolere possit his, qui ignorant, et errant. Quoniam et ipse circumdatus est infirmitate, propterea debet, quemadmodum pro populo, ita etiam pro semetipso offerre pro peccatis (Heb. V, 1). Et mox id ipsum explanans: Sicut Aaron, ita etiam Christus (Ibid., 5). Deinde ostendens assumptae naturae infirmitatem dicit: Qui in diebus carnis suae preces supplicationesque ad eum, qui potens est ipsum servare a morte, cum clamore valido et lacrymis offerens, exauditus est pro pietate. Et quidem cum esset Filius, didicit ex quibus passus est, obedientiam, et consummatus factus est omnibus obedientibus sibi causa salutis aeternae, appellatus a Deo pontifex secundum ordinem Melchisedech (Ibid., 7).

Quis igitur virtutis laboribus consummatus est, cum non esset natura perfectus? Quis est, qui experimentis didicit obedientiam, quam ante experimentum nesciebat? Quis est qui cum reverentia vixit? Quis cum clamore valido et lacrymis supplicationes offerens, et servare seipsum non valens, sed eum, qui servare possit, obsecrans, et liberationem mortis expetens? Non Deus Verbum, immortale, impassibile, incorporale: Cujus commemoratio, secundum Prophetam, laetificatio est, et levatio lacrymarum; ipse enim absterget omnem lacrymam ab omni vultu (Isa. XXV, 9, sec. LXX). Et rursus Propheta: Memor fui, inquit, Dei (Psal. LXXVI, 4), et laetatus sum, quod coronat pietate praeclaros (Dan. XIII, 2); quod omnia Patris possidet (Joan.

XVI, 15); quod est imago simillima genitoris (Coloss. I, 15, 39); quod in se Patrem ostendit (Joan. XIV, 10): sed magis, quod ex semine David a Deo fuerat assumptum, mortale et passibile; quod pavit ad mortem, licet ipsum postea imperium mortis destruxerit, propter assumentis divinitatem; quod per omnem justitiam ambulavit; quod ad Joannem dixit: Sine modo, decet nos implere omnem justitiam (Matth. III, 15); quod pontificatus appellationem accepit secundum ordinem Melchisedech (Heb. V, 10): ipsum enim portabat naturae infirmitatem, non item omnipotens Deus Verbum. Ideo et ante beatus dixerat Paulus: Non enim habemus pontificem, qui non possit condolere infirmitatibus nostris; tentatum autem in omnibus ad similitudinem absque peccato (Heb. IV, 15).

Haec tota fere περικοπὴ in V synodo legitur collat. 6: contendunt vero Theodoretus et Cyrillus hoc in loco magna vi argumentorum, sed majore studio partium: agitur enim, quod non semel monui, causa Procli, quem invisum Theodoretus, utpote Nestorii adversarium nobilem; charum Cyrillus, velut ducem pugnantium pro fide Constantinopoli, habebat. Cyrillo conversionem Verbi in carnem Theodoretus objicit, Cyrillus contra exprobrat deflendam amentiam, ignorantiam mysterii quo de agitur, assertionem ἑνώσεως σχετικῆς, consensionem cum Nestorio, impietatem et contradictionem. Tota ista Cyrilli oratio magnam crucem figere potest Theodoreti patronis.

Experta est autem passiones nostras, absque peccato, natura illa, quae ex nobis pro nobis assumpta est; non qui eam pro salute nostra assumpsit. Et in principio hujus capituli iterum docet: Considerate apostolum et pontificem confessionis nostrae Jesum, fidelem ei, qui fecit ipsum, sicut et Moyses in omni domo sua (Heb. III, 1). Facturam autem quis esse umquam dixerit recta sentiens, increatum, et cum Patre coaeternum Deum Verbum; sed eum, qui ex semine David, qui, liber ab omni peccato, pontifex noster fuit, victimam ipse se pro nobis offerens Deo, habens in se certe Dei Verbum adunatum sibi et inseparabiliter conjunctum?

RESPONSIO ORTHODOXI.

Jeremias propheta cum Israel offendisset Deum, eumque ad iracundiam provocasset, contristatus dicebat: Quis dabit capiti meo aquam, et oculis meis fontem lacrymarum, ut possim deflere populum hunc dies et noctes (Jerem. IX, 1)? Et ego opinor voces hujusmodi, non Israeli magis convenire, quam iis, qui patulum semper et petulcum os habent in Christum: Qui etiam ineffabili detrahunt gloriae, audaces, petulantesque (II Petr. II, 10), juxta quod scriptum est. Fletu autem sunt et lamentatione dignissimi, qui infinita dementia rectam et inculpabilem pietatis in Christum semitam negligentes, distortam orbitam, ambagesque sectantur, et cogitationum pravis inventis decus inquinant veritatis.

Ergo audiant, qui invisa omnibus sentiunt, errantes in scientia Scripturarum, nescientes magnum et venerabile Incarnationis mysterium: divinae enim Scripturae, hominem similem nobis factum fuisse praedicant Emmanuel, et participasse carni et sanguini, similiter ac nos, Verbum Dei et Patris. Affirmant et carnem factum, id est, hominem; non per conversionem, aut per commutationem, sed virtute adunationis arcanae, proptereaque unum dicimus Jesum Christum Dominum, et unam fidem, unum item sanctum baptisma.

Hi vero a rectis dogmatibus abhorrentes, et adversus sacras litteras durum sensum insolentemque opponentes; ad id tantummodo, quod ipsis bene habere videtur, inspiciunt, et hominem assumptum a Deo Verbo commemorant, juxta illud fortasse quod ab uno prophetarum dictum est: Propheta non eram, nec filius Prophetae; sed pastor eram vellicans sycomora; et assumpsit me Deus ex ovibus (Amos VII, 14); aut forte, sicut ait beatus David: Assumens mansuetos Dominus (Psal. CXLVI, 6); secundum σχέσιν scilicet et familiaritatem spiritalem, quam voluntate, et gratia, et sanctificatione, nos etiam habemus ipsi: adhaerentes enim Domino, unus spiritus sumus, juxta quod scriptum est (I Cor. VI, 17). Id autem nequaquam significat, Deum hominem fuisse factum; neque eum similiter ac nos, participasse carni et sanguini, sed magis assumpsisse hominem, non alio pacto, quam quo dicitur, et apostolos, et prophetas, et omnes alios sanctos assumpsisse.

Decipitne divinus Paulus sanctificatos per fidem, evidentissime de Unigenito dicens, quod cum dives esset, pauper est factus (II Cor. VIII, 9)? Absit:

numquam enim mentietur veritatis maximus praedicator. Sed quisnam sit dives, et quomodo pauper sit factus, nunc quoque diligentius perscrutemur. Etenim si, ut illi dicere et sentire confidunt, homo est assumptus a Deo; quomodo is qui assumptus est a Deo, factus est pauper, cum sublimioribus naturae suae dignitatibus illustratus sit? glorificatus est enim. At si id verum non est, reprehendetur ab ipsis assumptio, quippe quae ad inferiorem, et ingloriosiorem dejecerit humanitatis modum. Verum ita sentire ineptum est. Ergo non is, qui assumptus est, pauper est factus; superest igitur, ut dicamus, Deum Verbum, cum esset dives, ad nostram pauperiem devenisse.

Verum quomodo pauper est factus? Age, ut necessarium est, attendamus: inconvertibilis quidem est procul dubio per naturam, nec sua derelicta, in naturam transiit carnis; permansit enim id quod erat, id est, Deus. Ubi igitur humilitatem videbimus paupertatis? In eone, quod unum similem nostri Deus assumpserit, sicut dicere ausi sunt impietatis Nestorii parasiti? Et quis fiat ipsi paupertatis et exinanitatis modus? In eone tantum, quod forte voluerit aliquem nostri similem hominem honorare? At nullo pacto beneficia praestando Deus omnipotens violatur: quomodo ergo pauper est factus? Quia cum esset Deus natura, et Filius Dei et Patris, factus est homo ex semine David; natus est secundum carnem, et servilem subiit mensuram, id est, humanam, qui est opifex omnium: homo enim factus, humanitatis non erubescit subire mensuram. Qui enim non recusavit esse similis nostri, quomodo ea recusaret, per quae hominem se nostri similem vere factum esse, posset ostendere? Si igitur eum ab humanis, et rebus, et sermonibus submoveamus, nullo pacto differimus ab his, qui eum, si fieri posset, sua carne etiam spoliarent; qui Scripturae divinae non credunt, evertentes omnino Incarnationis mysterium, salutem orbis terrarum, spem, fidem, resurrectionem.

Dicat aliquis, Deo Verbo parum decorum esse, et nullo modo conveniens, lacrymari, timere mortem, calicem recusare, subire officium sacerdotis. Valde ego quoque libens assentiam, haec divinae naturae et gloriae minime convenire. Verumtamen in his video paupertatem, quam propter nos volens ipse sustinuit. Si tibi gravis videatur exinanitatis injuria, eo plus mirare erga nos Filii charitatem; quod enim tam indecorum dicis, et parvum, hoc Deus tui causa sibi fecit amabile.

More hominum lacrymavit, ut tuas lacrymas ipse cohiberet. Expavit dispensatorie permittens carni interdum pati, quae sua sunt, ut nos confidentissimi redderemur. Calicem recusavit, ut crux impietatem argueret Judaeorum. Infirmatus esse dicitur secundum humanitatem, ut te infirmitatibus liberaret. Preces supplicationesque obtulit, ut tuis etiam supplicationibus aurem facilem redderet, ut tu disceres in tentationibus minime dormitare, sed animum orationibus magis intendere. Ideoque dormitantes sanctos apostolos incusabat dicens: Sic non potuistis una hora vigilare mecum? vigilate et orate, ne intretis in tentationem (Matth. XXVI, 4). Se enim tamquam reformationem vitae beatae praebens, profuit mundo; ideo humanitatis infirmitates familiares fecit ut etiam vere homo factus esse crederetur, cum permansisset nihilominus id quod erat, id est, Deus.

Sed nescio quomodo hi, qui Christum se unum dicere simulant, et Filium, et Dominum, eumdemque Deum simul et hominem, dicunt, non Dei Verbum nuncupatum fuisse pontificem, et apostolum confessionis nostrae, tunc cum factus est homo; sed aut alium, nescio quem, seorsus hominem ipsum per se, qui erat ex semine David, in id vocatum esse affirmant: forsitan metuentes, ne si recta sentiant, ab impietate videantur Nestorii defecisse. Ait enim hoc modo ille (Serm. 6 qui tertius in Proclum): Hic, qui fidelis ad Deum pontifex factus est; factus est enim, et non semper fuerat; hic, qui paulatim in pontificis profecit, haeretice, dignitatem. Deinde, ut ipse existimat, suarum vocum cupiens veritatem confirmare, dicit: De quo et Lucas in Evangeliis clamabat: Jesus autem proficiebat aetate, et sapientia, et gratia. Et rursus: Sed cum sit nobis hic solus pontifex condolens, et cognatus, et certus, ab ipsius natura non seducamini: ipse enim nobis ex promissa benedictione et semine Abrahae missus est, pro se ipso, et suo genere corporis victimam secum adducens.

At dementiae illius optimus aemulator, vir bonus Theodoretus, non erubescit dicens: Humanam naturam assumpsit, et eam super communes pontifices ordinavit, sicut et Paulus dicit: Omnis enim pontifex ex hominibus assumptus pro hominibus constituitur in his, quae sunt ad Deum, qui condolere possit his, qui ignorant et errant, quoniam et ipse circumdatus est infirmitate; et propterea debet, quemadmodum pro populo, ita etiam pro semetipso offerre pro peccatis. Nonne hominem nobis communem Emmanuel, quantum ad ipsum pertinet, effecit? Nonne supra memoratis haec quoque sunt germanae sententiae, eamdem blasphemiam parturientes? Quid ais? Metuis sacerdotii modum in Christo omnium salvatore; nec conveniens videtur esse Deo Verbo humano more ministrare, propter dispensationem? Detege tuum vultum, persona deposita, et palam denega Dei Verbi incarnationem, propter quam et pontifex nominatus est. Immolantemne eum conspicis, tamquam alii et majori Deo, Patri? Contemplatusne es sacrificia offerentem, exemplo eorum qui ab hominibus assumpti sunt, quique condolere possunt ignorantibus et errantibus, ideo quod et ipsi sint in infirmitatibus nostris? An non considerasti, quod fidem omnium, sive fidei confessionem, et Spiritui sancto consecrat et Patri? hicne humani ministerii modus est poscere fidem ab his, qui in odorem suavitatis oblati sint in spiritu? Animadverte, quam diverso modo, cum Deus sit, licet humano more, propter dispensationem ministrare dicatur: considet enim Deo et Patri, et in sedibus excelsis conspicitur. Terret te quod humanitatis, nec te quod divinitatis, liberat metu? Non pateris, ex rebus ipsis inspicere, Deum esse simul et hominem Emmanuel; sed tam petulanter et inconsiderate, immo ultra terminos impietatis totius excurrens, ais ipsum consummatum esse laboribus, et virtute, et profecisse paulatim in pontificis dignitatem. Si profecit, ubi exinanitas, et ubi pauper est factus? Si consummatus est per virtutem, ex imperfecto utique, et in tempore factus est perfectus. Quidquid autem non est in virtute perfectum, culpa et vitio continetur; et quod vitio continetur, in peccato est. Quomodo igitur de ipso scriptum est, quod peccatum non fecit (I Petr. II, 22)?

Ausus est dicere, quae infra scripta: Quis igitur sacerdos est factus? Quis virtute consummatus est, cum non esset natura perfectus? Quis tentationibus didicit obedientiam, quam ante tentationes nesciebat? Quis cum reverentia vixit, et cum clamore valido lacrymans, et supplicationes offerens, cum se servare non posset, sed eum, qui servare posset, obsecrans? O audacissimam et sceleratissimam vocem! quae lacrymae tam impie credentium poterunt abolere peccata? Si acquiescis adunationi, quomodo ignorasti, quod de Deo dicas, qui factus sit homo? Humiliavit se tua causa, et tu impie exclamas: Propitius esto, Domine, numquam tibi erit istud. Ergo audies ipsum dicentem: Vade retro a me, Satana; scandalum mihi es (Matth. XVI, 22).

Sed enim in clausula suorum dictorum dixit: Ergo is, qui ex semine David, pontifex est, habens in se scilicet Deum Verbum sibi adunatum, et inseparabiliter conjunctum. Et quomodo adunatum dicit Deo Verbo id, quod est ex semine David, si soli ei, qui est ex semine David, sacerdotium deputavit? Nam si vera est adunatio, non sunt duo omnino, sed unus, et solus, qui ex utrisque intelligitur Christus.

Certum est ergo, illos simulate adunationem confiteri, simpliciorum animos insectantes: conjunctionem namque credunt σχετικὴν, et extrinsecus factam, quam nos etiam habuimus, cum participes divinae ipsius naturae facti sumus per spiritum. Non adhaerendum igitur illorum vanitatibus, sed rectae et inculpabili fidei, et evangelicis, et apostolicis sanctionibus.

ANATHEMATISMUS UNDECIMUS.

Siquis non confiteatur carnem Domini vivificam esse, et ipsius Dei Verbi propriam, sed ut alterius cujuspiam, conjuncti quidem ipsi per dignitatem, sive per solam inhabitationem; ac non magis vivificam, ut ante dixi, eo quod sit propria Verbi, quod omnia potens est vivificare; anathema sit.

REPREHENSIO HAERETICI.

Quantum apparet, obscuritati studet, ut impietatem suam occultet, qui eadem cum haereticis sentit; sed nihil veritate validius, quae radiis suis mendacii potest caliginem revelare. Ea illuminati manifestam ejus fidem ἑτερόδοξον faciamus. Primum quidem, nusquam carnis rationabilis meminit, nec hominem perfectum, qui est assumptus, confessus est; sed ubique carnem dicit, Apollinaris sequens dogmata. Deinde, commixtionis opinionem, aliis eam vocibus proferens, aspergit sermonibus, hinc enim aperte inanimam dicit Domini carnem, cum ait: Si quis confiteatur Domini carnem non esse propriam ipsius Dei Verbi, sed ut alterius praeter ipsum, anathema sit. Unde apparet eum non confiteri Deum Verbum animam assumpsisse, sed carnem tantummodo; ipsum autem esse carni pro anima: nos vero vivificam dicimus, animatam, et rationabilem Domini carnem, propter adunatam ipsi vivificam deitatem.

Confitetur autem ipse quoque, licet invitus, differentiam naturarum, carnem nominans et Deum Verbum, et propriam ipsius dicens fuisse carnem: igitur non Deus Verbum in carnis naturam conversum est; sed propriam habet carnem, assumptam scilicet naturam, et vivificam eam adunatione effecit.

RESPONSIO ORTHODOXI.

Qui a rectis et veris cogitationibus per imperitiam delapsi sunt, pene etiam dicunt: Posuimus mendacium spem nostram, et mendacio operiemur (Isai. XXVIII, XV). In quemcumque enim ipsis libitum fuerit, proferunt inconsiderate sententiam; nec meminerunt divinae Scripturae dicentis: Judicium justum judicate (Zach. VII, 9). Et rursus: Testis falsus non erit impunitus (Prov. XIX, 5). Nos etenim vivificum esse dicimus sanctum corpus salvatoris omnium Christi. Est namque non unius simpliciter similis nostri hominis, et communis; proprium autem magis vere Verbi, quod omnia vivificat. Sic autem proprium, ut si forte dicatur uniuscujusque nostri proprium corpus suum.

Hic autem vir bellus, verbositatis suae in nos nullum modum praeteriit intentatum, quamvis nostris dictis consentiat. Inurit rursus nobis Apollinaris impietatis infamiam; nec erubescit, commemorans me verbis aliis, ac dictionibus, rem commixtionis sive confusionis occultare, et inanimam dicere carnem Verbo conjunctam. Sed dixerit ad eum forte aliquis: O vir optime, iisdem etiam beatum Joannem criminibus accusabis; ait enim: Verbum caro factum est (Joan. I, 14). Age igitur cum ipso etiam insolenter, et dic, animae eum non meminisse rationabilis, sed inanimam dicere Domini carnem. Quid si etiam ipsum dicere audieris Christum omnium salvatorem: Amen dico vobis, nisi manducaveritis carnem Filii hominis, et biberitis ipsius sanguinem, non habebitis vitam in vobis. Et rursus: Qui manducat carnem meam, et bibit sanguinem meum, in me manet, et ego in ipso. Et rursus: Panis autem, quem ego dabo, caro mea est pro mundi vita (Joan. VI, 54). Insulta, si videbitur, etiam ipsi Verbo: carnem enim nominat tantum, nec animae rationabilis in his facit usquam mentionem.

At tu, si sagax esses et sapiens, non ignorares quod plerumque etiam sola carnis mentione animal, quod est ex anima et corpore, designetur, id est, homo. Scriptum est enim: quod videbit omnis caro salutare Dei (Isai. XL, 5). Ergo qui carnem dicit fuisse factum Verbum, non ignorat omnino se etiam animae rationabilis facere mentionem. Verum, quod a principio dixi, in probationibus deficiens, invenit sibi mendacium tegumentum, et calumniari conatur, ut aliquid dicere videatur.

At vero, hominem assumptum fuisse a Deo, sanctis Patribus non videtur: Neque enim ita umquam crediderunt; sed ipsum magis Deum Verbum hominem factum esse dixerunt, adunatumque carni habenti animam rationabilem. Inconfusa autem, et absque conversione omnino est adunatio: inconvertibile est enim Dei Verbum, et ita credimus.

ANATHEMATISMUS DUODECIMUS.

Siquis non confiteatur quod Dei Verbum passum sit carne, et crucifixum carne, et mortem gustavit carne, et factum primogenitum ex mortuis, eo quod, ut Deus, det vitam, et sit vivificum; anathema sit.

REPREHENSIO HAERETICI.

Passiones naturae passibilis propriae sunt; impassibilis, passionibus superior est; passa est igitur servi forma, adhaerente ipsi scilicet etiam Dei forma, et permittente quidem pati, propter salutem, quae ex passionibus fuerat eventura; suas vero passiones, propter adunationem, dicente: ergo non Deus passus est, sed homo, qui ex nobis a Deo assumptus est. Propterea et beatus Isaias ante praenuntians, clamat: Homo in plaga, et sciens ferre infirmitatem (Isai. LIII, 3). Et ipse Dominus Christus ad Judaeos dicebat: Quid me quaeritis occidere hominem, qui veritatem vobis locutus sum (Joan. VIII, 40). Occiditur vero non ipsa vita, sed qui mortalem habet naturam. Et id alibi docens Dominus ad Judaeos dixit: Solvite templum istud, et in triduo reaedificabo ipsum. Ergo solutus quidem est, qui est ex David; resuscitavit vero solutum, unigenitum Deus Verbum, quod ex Patre impassibiliter ante saecula natum est.

RESPONSIO ORTHODOXI.

Est quidem impassibilis procul dubio Verbi natura, et id nulli est hominum, ut opinor, incertum. Neque enim ad tam insanam dementiam quisquam delabetur, ut illam arcanam et passionibus superiorem naturam dicat nostris infirmitatibus teneri. Sed quoniam passio mundo futura erat salutaris; erat autem impossibile, ut in sua natura Verbum Deus aliquid pateretur; dispensationem subiit sapienter: proprium enim corpus fecit, quod poterat pati, ut corpore patiente, ipse passus fuisse dicatur, licet ipse per suam naturam impassibilis permansisset.

Verum quoniam carne passus est volens, propterea omnium salvator, et est, et nominatur. Ut enim Paulus ait: Gratia Dei pro omnibus gustavit mortem (Heb. II, 9). Testatur vero etiam divinus Petrus sapientissime dicens: Christo ergo passo pro nobis (I Petr. IV, 1). Non deitatis utique natura, sed carne. Denique quonam modo Dominus gloriae crucifixus esse dicitur? quo item modo is, per quem omnia, et in quo omnia ordinata sunt (I Cor. II, 8; Heb. II, 10), ut ait beatus Paulus, datus est a Deo et Patre caput corporis Ecclesiae, factus primogenitus ex mortuis? carnis scilicet passiones familiariter passus; Dominus autem gloriae nequaquam fuit homo nostri similis et communis.

Sed forte dices sufficere unitatem ad probandum unum esse Christum et Dominum crucifixum. Ergo omnia dicantur ipsius, et credatur Dei Verbum esse Salvator, permanens quidem impassibile secundum deitatis naturam, carne autem passum, juxta quod dixit Petrus: ipsius enim erat proprium per veram adunationem corpus, quod mortem gustavit. Denique quomodo ex Judaeis secundum carnem Christus et Deus super omnes, et benedictus in saecula, amen (Rom. IX, 18). In cujus morte baptizati sumus? cujus resurrectionem confitentes justificamur? An hominis communis alicujus? An, quod verius est, Dei hominis facti et passi pro nobis carne, mortem denuntiamus, et confitentes resurrectionem, onus abjicimus peccatorum? Empti enim sumus pretio, non corruptibilibus argento vel auro; sed pretioso sanguine, sicut agni puri et immaculati, Christi (I Cor. VI, 20; I Petr. I, 19).

Plura quidem et alia super his commemorare, nihil difficile est, et sanctorum Patrum exempla proponere: verum haec satis fore opinor docilioribus; scriptum est enim: Da sapienti occasionem, et sapientior erit; annuntia justo, et adjiciet ad percipiendum (Prov. IX, 9).

Verba haec: PASSUS EST VOLENS, πέπονθεν ἔκων, exagitavit Eutherius sermone 8 quemadmodum et ista: VERBUM CARNE PASSUM EST, ἔπαθεν ὁ Θεὸς Λόγος σαρκί. Tanta porro est Eranistem inter et reprehensiones capitum, sive sententiarum affinitas, sive verborum similitudo, ut non tantum eumdem ostendant auctorem, quem nemo non agnoscit; sed eumdem quoque adversarium, quem pauci advertunt esse Cyrillum, quod tamen demonstrabimus, opinor, in auctario operum Theodoreti, quod apparamus, propediem, si fuerit Dei voluntas, prelo subdendum: eo enim in loco, post vitam Theodoreti suis actibus distinctam, post fidem discussam, judicium de singulis operibus ita instituetur, ut plura, quorum partem dedit Mercator, deesse in editione Sirmondiana probentur, singulorumque historia, id est, tempus, causae, qualitasque narretur.

The Scriptorium Project is the work of a small group of lay people of various apostolic churches who are interested in the preservation, transmission, and translation of the works of the early and medieval church. Our efforts are to make the works of the church fathers accessible to anyone who might have an interest in Christian antiquities and the theological, philosophical, and moral writings that have become the bedrock of Western Civilization.

To-date, our releases have pulled from the Greek, Syriac, Georgian, Latin, Celtic, Ethiopian, and Coptic traditions of Christianity, and have been pulled from sundry local traditions and languages.

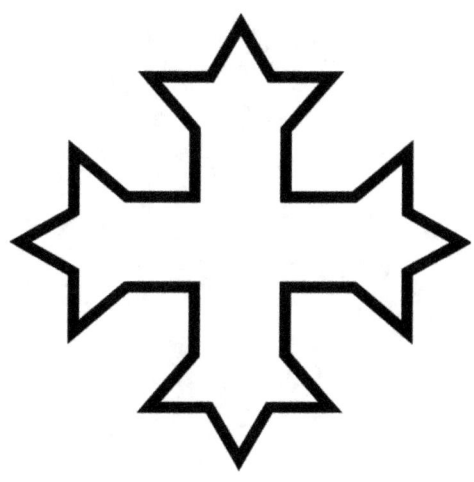

Nile River Valley Church Series (Coptic, Nubian, Ethiopian):

Apology Against Theodore by St. Cyril of Alexandria (Nov. 2009)

The Paradise of Heraclides by Heraclides of Alexandria (Apr. 2013)

Discourse on Mary Theotokos by St. Cyril of Jerusalem (Sept. 2013)

Nicene Canons in the Old Nubian Language (Jan. 2018)

First Book of Ethiopian Maccabees (Dec 2018)

Life of St. Mary the Egyptian by St. Sophronius of Jerusalem (May 2019)

The Old Nubian Miracle of St. Mena (Jan. 2021)

Two Letters by St. Dionysius of Alexandria (Apr. 2022)

Instructions: Counsel for Novices by St. Ammonas the Hermit (Sept 2022)

Religious Exercise and Quiet by St. Isaiah the Solitary (Oct 2022)

The Vision of Theophilus by St. Cyril of Alexandria (Dec 2022)

Second Book of Ethiopian Maccabees (Aug 2023)

www.ingramcontent.com/pod-product-compliance
Lightning Source LLC
LaVergne TN
LVHW010558070526
838199LV00063BA/5001